Sweetwater Sea Saga

Virginia M. Soetebier

The McDonald and Woodward Publishing Company
Blacksburg, Virginia
1991

The McDonald and Woodward Publishing Company
P. O. Box 10308, Blacksburg, Virginia 24062–0308

Sweetwater Sea Saga
© 1991 by The McDonald and Woodward Publishing Company

All rights reserved
Printed in the United States of America
by McNaughton & Gunn, Saline, Michigan
Composition by Marathon Typesetting, Roanoke, Virginia

10 9 8 7 6 5 4 3 2 1

First printing July 1991

Library of Congress Cataloging-in-Publication Data

Soetebier, Virginia M. (Virginia Marie), 1930–
    Sweetwater sea saga / Virginia M. Soetebier.
      p.   cm.   Includes bibliographical references.
    ISBN 0-939923-18-1 : $9.95
    1. Superior, Lake—Description and travel. 2. Sailing—Superior, Lake. 3. Superior, Lake, Region—Description and travel. 4. Soetebier, Virginia M. (Virginia Marie), 1930–3 Journeys—Superior, Lake. I. Title.
F552.S64 1991
917.74'90443—dc20
                                      91-13794
                                        CIP

Reproduction or translation of any part of this work, except for short excerpts used in reviews, without the written permission of the copyright owner is unlawful. Requests for permission to reproduce parts of this work, or for additional information, should be addressed to the publisher.

Dedication

For Jack.

Without him, there would have been no book.

Contents

Chapter 1	First Trip on the Inland Sea	1
Chapter 2	Crossings	9
Chapter 3	Apostle Islands Yacht Club	17
Chapter 4	Thunder Bay	29
Chapter 5	Silver Islet	41
Chapter 6	Otter Cove	51
Chapter 7	Rossport and Nipigon	55
Chapter 8	Isle Royale	69
Chapter 9	Ontonagon	81
Chapter 10	Black River Harbor	85
Chapter 11	From the Head of the Lake to the Foot of It	91
Chapter 12	Rescue in the Susie Islands	101
Postscript	Lake Superior	107

Who durst be so bold with a few crooked boards nailed together, a stick standing upright, and a rag tied to it, to adventure into the ocean?

Thomas Fuller, *The Good Sea Captain*

Although those words were written in the 17th century about the sea, I think they apply to the great Lake Superior, a true "inland sea."

Sweetwater Sea Saga

Chapter 1

First Trip on the Inland Sea

The first time I crossed Lake Superior (Figure 1) by boat I didn't dream that I would cross it some 30 times again in my life.

The first crossing was unique. We left Black River Harbor, Michigan, at midnight on the Saturday of Labor Day weekend 1948. The crew consisted of the Soetebier family—Alfred and Elsie, and sons Dick and Jack, along with Dick's girlfriend and I. The weather was mild, the seas were running two to three feet high, and the night was so black that one could easily sympathize with Columbus's men who thought they would sail off the edge of the earth if they ventured too far from land.

Although Jack's father owned the 38-foot Matthews motorboat cruiser *Viking*, Jack did most of the actual work aboard the craft. He was experienced in running a boat. During previous summer vacations from high school, he had taken day-long sport-fishing parties out on Lake Superior, trolling for lake trout on *Viking's* predecessor, the *Swan*. The 18-year-old captain, however, had no knowledge of compass deviation and magnetic

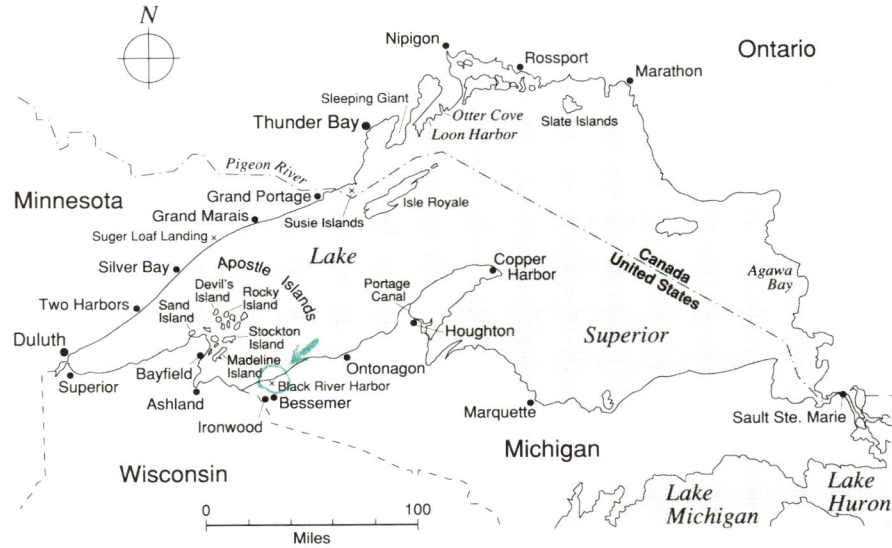

Figure 1. Lake Superior and its immediate environs.

variation on navigational charts. Dead reckoning was his system of navigation.

Accordingly, on that Labor Day weekend in 1948, Jack set forth from the sparsely-lit harbor and sailed by his boat compass northeast for Isle Royale, a place none of us had ever seen but of which all had heard (Figure 2). The midnight departure was not in deference to tide and current, as it might be on the seacoast. Rather, Jack simply felt it would be easier to see the island if we approached it in daylight rather than darkness.

By dawn's gray light, we could barely discern some dark, irregular lines to the west of our boat heading. All hands deduced that the darker gray humps were the island we were seeking and that we had gone too far east in the dark. So, we altered course to the west and travelled farther and farther in that direction. Every hour, the gray lines on the horizon became higher and higher hills. By late Sunday morning, the binoculars

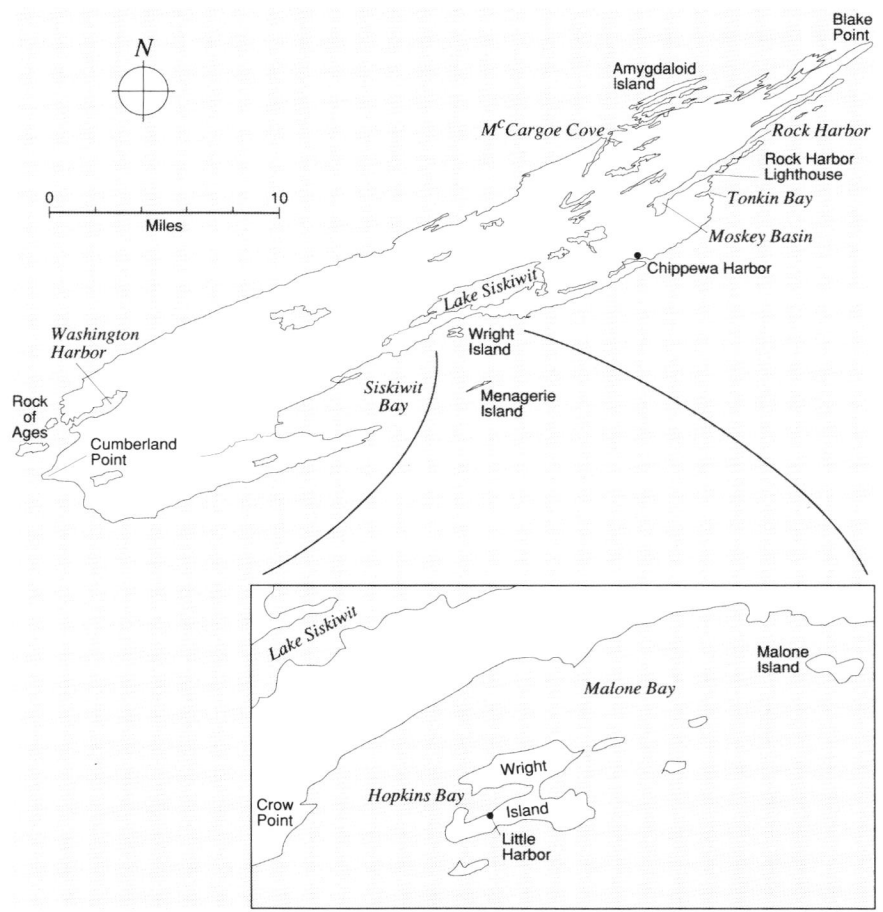

Figure 2. Isle Royale.

revealed that cars abounded on the now not-so-distant hills.

"I don't know where we are, but it's not Isle Royale. There are no cars on Isle Royale!" Jack's mom said. As usual, she was right.

We docked at Grand Marais, Minnesota, around noontime, and managed to get a gasoline tanker truck to come down to the Coast Guard dock and fill up the *Viking* with fuel.

Despite Jack's lack of navigational knowledge, we had been headed right for Isle Royale before we were lured off course by the faraway, seductive Sawtooth Mountains. The island is lower than the high hills behind it on the mainland, so we saw the higher land first and assumed that it was Isle Royale. If we had had a little more faith and continued on Jack's original course, the island soon would have appeared on our horizon and we would have hit Washington Harbor and Rock of Ages lighthouse right on the nose. Late Sunday, we did reach that very spot, where we tied up to a deserted fisherman's dock, stayed overnight, and spent the next day exploring nearby Singers Island, now called Washington Island.

On the shore was a tiny fishing village sporting a dozen or so buildings. An avenue led past one small house after another, all with flowers blooming on either side of the front doors. Beside each were wooden racks with fish nets drying on them. The village, however, appeared to be deserted. The residents were apparently moving their kids back to the mainland that weekend, getting them ready for the opening of school the following Tuesday. Even the National Park Service employees deserted Isle Royale by Labor Day in the 1940s. In fact, we failed to see even one of the vaunted moose of the island! Finally, however, a lone fisherman appeared and sold us enough gasoline to get home—at 50 cents a gallon—even though he needed it himself for fishing. Alfred and Elsie were shocked—gasoline sold for 25 cents a gallon in those days!

The *Viking's* trip home on Monday was rough—beam seas reached to five feet, the skies were again gray, and the weather was rainy. All of the crew except Jack's dad and I were seasick. Even our capable skipper curled up on the heaving bunk, neither eating nor drinking all the way across the lake. Alfred—son of Hamburg, Germany, that he always was—took the wheel all the way back to Black River Harbor. When he called for food, I cooked hamburgers, fried potatoes, and fried onions! Just the kind of odors the sufferers needed! It was dark again before we cleared the prominent red clay bluffs which mark the entrance to Black River Harbor.

Little did I know that this weekend journey was but a preview of what my summer vacations would be like for the next 40 years!

On my first crossing I learned that the waters of Lake Superior are cold, dark, deceptive, and unforgiving. Waves can be menacingly high one minute, serene and calm the next. I learned that if you fall off a boat in Superior, you won't float many miles on a piece of debris, as survivors of shipwrecks do on salty seas. This water is so pure it provides little natural buoyancy. And, I learned that a person will not survive for more than 20 minutes or so when immersed in Lake Superior. The water is numbingly cold anywhere beyond the merest fringes of the lake. Superior does not easily or gladly give up her dead. The bodies of those unfortunate enough to drown in this vast sea may never be seen again. I learned, on my first crossing, that this is a stern Mother Superior.

At that point in my life, my sixteenth summer, prospects real and imagined stretched before me—perhaps I would be a foreign correspondent stationed in Paris, or editor of a fashion magazine in New York. But life decreed instead that I should remain on the shores of this great lake, as housewife and mother. When a real opportunity to leave this part of the world was offered to me, to live permanently in Germany, I refused. I remained in this sacred place—considered by Ojibway Indians to be the center of the earth—for various personal reasons, but partly my decision was based on a physical and emotional need to be near these fascinating waters, surrounded by glorious forests. I've never regretted my decision.

My admiration for the hardy residents of Superior's shores, and those who worked upon her—voyageurs of the 18th century, fishermen of the 19th century, and ore-boat crews of the 20th century—has grown with my knowledge of the lake. Over the years, we found that we could go about as far in one day on our various sailboats and motorboats as the voyageurs had gone during a day of strenuous paddling, so nightly, on our summer cruises, guided by the reports of various writers and diarists, we stopped and camped in the same spots as had the travelers whose accounts we were reading. We always felt especially close to those early explorers and traders when we followed so closely in their wakes. All the history of the area is captivating—possible visits by Vikings, religious rites of Native Americans, the lore of life on the lake in the historic period. The awe which I first felt during that late summer voyage on the *Viking* as we bounced from wave to wave in utter darkness, no object to be seen in any direction, remains with me to this day.

My first crossing of this magnificent, indifferent, capricious body of water gave me a taste for the unsalted sea, a taste still unsatiated.

Jack and I married in 1951; since then we've had five children and five boats. Our first boat was a fiberglass-over-wood dingy that Jack built in our laundry room; it was powered by an outboard motor. By the time we had Kurt, Lynn, and Laura, we owned the *Möwe*, a one-of-a-kind 25-foot wooden sloop. When Gretchen arrived, so did sailboat racing and the sloop *Blitzen*, a fiberglass Columbia 29. After Heidi was born, the 360-mile Trans-Superior Race began and we needed a 34-foot Ericson fiberglass sloop, *Hussar*. Now that it's just the two of us again, we enjoy the comfort of our 38-foot steel-hulled Chris Craft Roamer, *Flying Dutchman*.

We spent our first 30 years on sailboats looking for ice for our icebox. Now that we have a powerboat with refrigerator and ice cubes, we're spending our second 30 years of boating looking for gasoline to keep the engines, and the generators, going.

Chapter 2

Crossings

In the 40 years that we have been sailing Lake Superior, we have crossed her at least twice each summer. We've gone in every kind of weather imaginable—clear, sunny, cold, hazy, and down-right foggy. We've crossed with not much wind and with the wind behind us, on our quarter, and head on. We even sailed once for nine hours on a broad reach from Rock Harbor, Isle Royale, to the entrance to Michigan's Portage Canal on the Keweenaw waterway, without ever changing sails or heading! Usually, the seas ran about two feet, often they were much higher, and only once or twice did we move through water still as glass. On one occasion, we sailed across when the outside temperature was 45 degrees F.

Most of the time we sailed across this "eighth sea," but now in our mid-life search for comfort and convenience, we motor across on the *Flying Dutchman*. Over the years, we've gone in every conceivable direction— from Washington Harbor on Isle Royale to the Apostle Islands; from Chippewa Harbor on Isle Royale to Grand Marais, Minnesota; from various spots along the North

Shore to Duluth; from Copper Harbor, Michigan, to Rock Harbor on Isle Royale; from Duluth to Sault Ste. Marie, Michigan. Our route purposely changed from year to year to allow the crews, bringing their boats to the International Sailboat Race or, returning them home afterward, to visit a different part of the great lake each summer.

For 23 years, Jack raced our various sailboats in every International Sailboat Race held on Lake Superior and, three times, he took part in the Trans-Superior Race (Figure 3). His racing crew consisted of some five or six hardy male sailors. Our children and I would meet the racers at the finish line; then our family would cruise the Isle Royale area, the mainland shore of Ontario, or the beautiful islands in the Rossport-Slate Islands area before heading home across the lake. Meanwhile, the

Figure 3. The racing fleet prior to the start of the 1971 Trans-Superior Race, from Sault Ste. Marie, Michigan, to Duluth, Minnesota, a distance of 390 miles. (Jack Soetebier photograph.)

crewmen would have driven home in our car from wherever the race ended.

Crossing Lake Superior has never been easy. We have always tried to cross in good weather, but sudden changes in the weather occur, often without warning. In the days before sophisticated weather forecasting, we might start out in fair weather and end up in heavy weather. In our time, we had to tough out many a bad day on the lake. Furthermore, it's a long trip, even in a powerboat. The narrowest crossing we've ever made was 50 miles, the widest more than 100 miles; top speed on our sailboats was between five and seven miles per hour.

More information on weather conditions became available when the National Weather Service began broadcasting MAFOR (*ma*rine *for*ecasts) bulletins. Using the data, however, made us feel like spies, since the information was broadcast in coded numbers and we would have to decode it. I always hated to see nines in a MAFOR bulletin since they indicated vile weather.

Today, the National Oceanic and Atmospheric Agency (NOAA) Weather Service has data buoys scattered across the lake which continuously collect such weather information as velocity and direction of the wind, and even heights of the waves. Since October, 1970, NOAA has broadcast this information continuously on a single weather station and, consequently, has aided the small-boat sailor on Lake Superior considerably. We rely heavily on the NOAA broadcasts.

When we changed from a sailboat to a powerboat, we gained usable space aboard, and we invested in some dandy navigational equipment. Under sail, it had been my job in a fog to blow into a hand-held brass horn every few minutes, but we now have an automatic fog horn. *Flying Dutchman* has an automatic pilot, which steers a straight course without so much as a touch of the hand, and a Raytheon radar set, which reports on a screen objects it "sees" in the dark or fog within a distance of 20 miles. Our radar has even picked up seagulls!

The best of all our modern devices, however, is loran (*lo*ng *ra*nge *n*avigation). This almost pocket-sized computerized direction finder is a marvelous navigational aid. By means of three powerful radio transmitters ashore, it can tell the boat's course, speed made good, distance to destination, and the latitude and longitude of present position.

The first season after we had purchased the loran, Jack plotted a course on it through very dangerous shoals north of Walker's Channel, east of Silver Islet, Ontario. We had to get off the lake as fast as possible because violent thundershowers, and their attendant winds, were being forecast. The fog had been so thick that, from the time we left Saganash Island until we saw the evergreen treetops in Walker's Channel, we had not been able to see one thing. We tied up at Saunders's dock just as the lightning began.

My most memorable crossing was in August 1970. After the International Sailboat Race, we cruised in the company of the Dr. John Pierpont family, first around the Thunder Bay, Ontario, area and then over to Isle Royale. Some combination of the Pierpont's seven sons and one daughter was aboard their 41-foot sloop *Siskiwit*, while our teenage daughters were with us on *Blitzen*.

When our two boats left Cumberland Point, Isle Royale, together, the forecast was for a cloudy day, but stormy or heavy weather was not anticipated. As we set our course and sails for the Apostle Islands, *Siskiwit* quickly sailed out of sight into a fog, not to be seen again on that trip. We tried to reach Piper—Dr. Pierpont—on our radio all day, but apparently his radio was not working.

When *Blitzen* approached the upbound steamer lanes in the heavy fog, Jack issued a security call on our

Figure 4. Pulpwood, after having been rafted across Lake Superior, being loaded onto rail cars for shipment to mills in Wisconsin. (From a postcard in the author's collection.)

marine radio, as he always does under such circumstances—two sailboats were on a course from the western end of Isle Royale to Outer Island in the Apostle Islands, and were moving at about six miles per hour. Shortly thereafter we talked to the skipper of the *John L. Roen III*, a tugboat pulling a log boom across the lake from Grand Marais, Minnesota, to Ashland, Wisconsin (Figure 4). Since our courses could have converged, we exchanged positions and kept in touch with the tug for the duration of that crossing. In addition to watching out in the fog for "salties" and iron-ore freighters, we also had to watch for a low-lying raft of slow-moving logs.

The *Roen* had excellent navigational equipment; the captain kept us in sight on his radar and talked to us frequently on his powerful radio. As *Blitzen* entered the downbound steamer lanes, still in the fog, and as the gray afternoon became a black evening, we could hear the repeated security calls from the skipper of the *Roen* to approaching ore boats in both lanes—he carried on conversations with the captains and mates of the ships out in the fog as if they were old friends as, indeed, perhaps they were. But, every transmission was concluded with the words, "Watch out for two sailboats, Cap, crossing your course, heading for the Apostle Islands." We may not have been able to see the behemoths of the lake, but, surely, thanks to the skipper of the *Roen*, the crews probably watched their radar screens a little more carefully and were more likely to have "seen" us.

The log boom being pulled by the *Roen* was one of the last to cross the lake. Consolidated Paper, Inc., shipped their last pulpwood in this fashion in August 1972. For 50 years, pulpwood had tumbled into the waters at Sugar Loaf Landing on the coast of Minnesota, there assembled and corralled by a huge fence of sitka spruce timbers fastened together with chains. Each of these rafts contained between 3,000 and 4,000 cords of wood, and filled 150 to 175 gondola rail cars at the South Shore port in Wisconsin; from there the wood was trans-shipped to Consolidated Paper's mills. A tugboat pulled the nest of floating logs across the lake at a speed of about two miles-per-hour. From the bow of the tug to the end of the raft, where a tender boat served as a navigational aid, was a distance of about one mile.

On our summer cruise of 1989, we traveled more calm, mirror-like water than we had seen in all of our years on Lake Superior. When we left Rock Harbor on Isle Royale for the entrance to the Portage Canal on the Keweenaw waterway, there was not a ruffle on the lake save for those in *Dutchman's* wake. But about a mile out, we ran into fog. There were record-breaking hot temperatures on the mainland, and the sun was bright above the fog, but the cold waters of the lake provided a thick and wet cloud around us for the entire crossing of 60 miles.

As we neared the upbound steamer lanes, Jack issued his usual security call and was answered immediately on the radio by a female voice. "This is *Columbia Star, Flying Dutchman*. How long are you?" Usually, when a woman is on the air on the lake, it's because her husband is busy taking fish off the line.

Jack replied that we were a 38-foot power boat and inquired about the length of the *Columbia Star*.

"One thousand feet" was the answer. Then the woman added that the *Columbia Star* was being followed by another ore boat. After we exchanged loran positions, we discovered that *Columbia Star* could not see the *Dutchman* on her radar, nor could we see *Columbia Star* on ours. This circumstance was disconcerting to us, but shortly, using loran positions, we determined the location of the *Columbia Star* in the fog and her movement in a direction away from us. Presently, another blip—the ore boat following *Columbia Star*—appeared on the other end of the screen. We were between the two boats but were moving safely enough away from both of them. When we got closer to the Keweenaw Peninsula, the fog lifted; we saw the trailing boat, but we never saw *Columbia Star* with our own eyes.

Chapter 3

The Apostle Islands Yacht Club

Apostle Islands Yacht Club! The name conjures up navy-blazered men in white bucks and white pants, standing on the fantail of a luxurious boat, holding glasses filled with iced beverages. And, the name itself is biblical, like names associated with the elegant sailing areas of Cape Cod and Newport—Martha's Vinyard, Point Judith, Galilee. But the reality of the early years of the Apostle Islands Yacht Club was very different from such an image.

Some people are addicted to large bodies of water, to sailing, and to boats of all kinds. Dr. John Pierpont is one of these people; my husband Jack is another.

Dr. Pierpont is a remarkable man who figures large in the recent sailing lore around Lake Superior. We first met Dr. Pierpont—now known to us as Piper or Doc—at Siskiwit Bay on Isle Royale in August 1953. We had arrived at Siskiwit Bay on the *Viking*. Doc was aboard the ketch *Northern Flight*; he had built her himself over a period of seven years at his home in Montreal, Wisconsin. Doc, his 13-year-old son Dave, and several friends were trying the then-excellent fishing on Siskiwit Lake.

By 1956, Doc had imported a beautiful new 41-foot Swedish-built sloop, *Siskiwit*, and sold *Northern Flight* to Oscar Swee, formerly a high school band director from Hurley, Wisconsin, who still sails her. We owned *Möwe* (Figure 5), which had been built only a block from our home on Park Point, for George Barnum III. *Möwe* had been proven a seaworthy craft; Barnum had sailed her annually to his family's summer home on Isle Royale for a number of years. In August, as Jack sailed *Möwe* off Bayfield, Wisconsin, in the heart of what is now the Apostle Islands National Lakeshore, he was challenged by the members of the fledgling Apostle Islands Yacht Club to join them in a race—and join them he did! Bill Peet of St. Paul, Minnesota, and Madeline Island, Wisconsin, triumphed in his open sloop *Bird*. Jack finished last in his first ever sailboat race; his record soon improved.

We were invited to the Apostle Islands Yacht Club's annual meeting held the next January in Swee's Hurley home during a raging snowstorm. The club had been formed primarily because John Pierpont wanted to compete in the world-famous Mackinac sailboat races and membership in a yacht club was a prerequisite. A constitution of 25 words or less was adopted and officers were elected: Commodore—Pierpont; Vice-Commodore—Swee; Secretary-Treasurer—Peet. Rufe Jefferson, another boat addict of the first water, had constructed a finely-detailed model of the *Corsair,* J. Pierpont Morgan's yacht, and he presented it to the group for use as a trophy for the winner of the Apostle Islands Yacht Club long distance sailing races-to-be.

The first long distance race sponsored by the Apostle Islands Yacht Club was held in 1957. It began off the city dock at Bayfield. Oscar Swee in *Northern Flight* was

Figure 5. *Möwe*, our 25-foot wooden sloop. (Jack Soetebier photograph.)

the first to finish at Washington Harbor, Isle Royale. Rufe Jefferson finished second in *Bluebird*, an unusual boat Jefferson had built at his home in Wayzata, Minnesota. *Bluebird's* hatch cover could be separated from the rest of the boat in an emergency to serve as a dingy. During the 80-mile race, Jefferson's only crew member was Geoffrey Pope whose left leg at the time was in a cast from thigh to toe! (Geoff later owned and sailed the *Sheila Yates* on Lake Superior and in the North Atlantic. *Sheila Yates* was a 50-foot square-sailed topsail ketch, built in Nova Scotia. She sank on her way to Cornwall, England, in the summer of 1989 while being towed away from a threatening field of pack ice.)

In July of 1959, the first island-to-island race in the Apostle Islands chain—eventually called the Inter-Island Race—was held in lieu of a long distance race. Bill and Barbara Peet won this race in *Bird II*, a beautifully-shaped craft but one without a cabin.

The first leg of the race was from Bayfield to Sand Island, at the western end of the Apostle Islands, where we were welcomed by the Bill Huling family. This was my first experience with private preservation of an historic site. The Anderson family, Mrs. Huling's parents and grandparents, had owned Sand Island for more than a century and had kept every building of the former fishing village in careful repair. No building had been modernized. The logs of the cabins had weathered to a soft gray inside and out; the floors were uneven wood planks, solid and shiny clean. Kerosene lamps lit the night. The outhouse was spotless. A Sunday morning religious service conducted by Mrs. Huling's father included a reading of scripture and singing of hymns, accompanied by a pump organ. The Anderson-Huling family was the finest of stewards; the National Park Service, which has taken over Sand Island as part of the Apostle Islands National Lakeshore, will be hard put to provide the same loving care.

Figure 6. The racing fleet docked at Rocky Island in the Apostle Islands, during the first Inter-Island Race held by the Apostle Island Yacht Club. (Jack Soetebier photograph.)

From Sand Island, the participants raced around Devil's Island and spent the night on Rocky Island (Figure 6). All slept aboard the boats, save the Peets, who had had the favor of a Huling cabin the night before and now rented one of the "hay fever haven" cabins of Rocky Island. Mrs. Nourse, who managed the small resort, provided all crews with what was to become our standard and eagerly-anticipated dinner—fried fresh lake trout, boiled potatoes, and lemon meringue pie!

The Peets had a most interesting crew member on this race. Ascetic Bill W. owned a kayak in which he paddled about the islands alone, so he was well prepared for the spartan life aboard the open-to-all-elements *Bird II*. His entire wardrobe for the four-day race consisted of shorts, shirt, sandals, and raincoat. He slept on Rocky Island in a hammock suspended between two huge fir trees on the shore. This fellow was a vegetarian; his main diet on the race was yogurt and whole wheat bread which he had made from grain he had ground himself. Soon after this race, he went to serve as a volunteer at a church mission in a remote village in Zaire.

Our last stop on the Inter-Island race of 1959 was Stockton Island, sometimes called Presque Isle. That night we began a tradition, well loved by our children, of a bonfire and sing-along on the beach on the last night of the race. Some crew member or another had brought along a guitar, and all of the participants in the race joined in the singing.

Canadians Ron Thomson and Jim Coslett joined the Apostle Islands Yacht Club for the Inter-Island race in 1961. They had just built a 28-foot Herreschoff ketch called *Windward* (Figure 7). The *Windward's* sea trials consisted of the 150-mile crossing of Lake Superior from Thunder Bay to Sand Island. Ron and Jim, and other of their countrymen have been coming across the lake ever since to compete with Apostle Islands Yacht Club members. In that easy way an international tradition began which later evolved into the International Sailboat Race.

The International Sailboat Race on Lake Superior, which officially began in 1965, was planned more for the fun of the sailors than for cut-throat competition. The race course was different nearly every year. One year it began at Isle Royale and went to the Apostle Islands, another year it started in the Apostle Islands and ended in Duluth, in yet another it went from Grand Marais, Minnesota, to Thunder Bay. It became customary for the race to end in a port in the United States one year and in Thunder Bay the next, a practical tradition that allowed those crew members cruising a boat to the starting point, or bringing home a boat after the race, to experience a variety of Lake Superior's scenery and harbors. It was a great tradition; Jack got to race his boat of the year, our family got to see the lake, and we all enjoyed our summer vacations. The Trans-Superior

Figure 7. Ron Thomson and Jim Coslett aboard the *Windward*, the ketch they built together, at Sand Island in the Apostle Islands. (Jack Soetebier photograph.)

Race, from Sault Ste. Marie, Michigan, to Duluth was first run in 1969 and has been raced every other year since. This 400-mile race considerably enlarged our cruising area!

Our young family, at that time a son and three daughters, raced with us during the early years of the Inter-Island Race—almost always held on the 4th of July weekend. Jack fretted that the kids were missing the customary fireworks, so one year he bought $100 worth of rockets, shooting stars, and roman candles. After dark, with the help of the teenage boys taking part in the race, he set off a spectacular fireworks display from the dock. I can recall the scene clearly. Most of the boats were anchored out for the night on the dark, still water. The fireworks were colorful against the dark sky and even darker evergreens along the shore. And, from aboard Frank Gokey's *Mimi L*, came a memorable sound! A crewman, who could not bear to be separated from his tuba, had taken it along on the races. With every brilliant visual explosion came an explosion of sound—runs, hoots, toots, and snatches of song! Kids young and old, on every boat there assembled, remember the 4th of July of 1966 as one of the best of their lives.

In 1964, Stockton Island was once again the scene of an unforgettable event. A commercial fisherman based on the island must surely have had a Scandinavian predecessor, for at the water's edge there stood a long-unused, small, mossy-roofed log cabin—a typical sauna. On the last day of the race, Salisbury Adams of Minneapolis inspired the teenage boys to accumulate great piles of driftwood on the beach near the sauna. At dusk, under Salisbury's direction, the boys started a huge fire, heated the beach rocks in it, and carried them into the little house in buckets. Then they poured cold lake water over the fiery rocks, creating a healthy steam. After a suitable length of time in the sauna, each teenager dove into the icy lake—the experience completed.

As our family grew, so did the size of our boats! After Gretchen came our 29-foot *Blitzen* (Figure 8). Heidi brought *Hussar* to us (Figure 9).

In 1963, the Apostle Islands Yacht Club had purchased a fisherman's property in the town of Bayfield to serve as a permanent home. The property consisted of one side of long, very sheltered slip with three or four buildings in various stages of disrepair. The club members faced the dock with sheet piling, extended finger piers outward into the slip, and demolished several small sheds. We put the best building into service as a clubhouse; we painted it and fitted it out with donated chairs, tables, couches, and drapes. Later, the highest fish house was remodeled into men's and women's bathrooms, with showers.

In those days, most members were raising families and had little extra income for boat-related expenses; so

Figure 8. *Blitzen*, our 29-foot Columbia fiberglass sloop. (Jack Soetebier photograph.)

Figure 9. *Hussar*, our 35-foot Ericson fiberglass sloop. (Jack Soetebier photograph.)

they gave their labor in the efforts to remodel the clubhouse. One spring weekend had been designated painting time for all hands. We stood on ladders, paint brushes in hand, but John Pierpont began loading his boat, even though no race had been scheduled. We questioned him and discovered that his oldest son, Dave, then a medical student, had only this one weekend free all summer. So father and son aimed for their beloved Isle Royale, *Siskiwit* sailed off into the sunrise, and Gene Meyer admonished us workers of the world to arise.

    The clubhouse soon became the locale of an annual Labor Day feast. Since few club members lived in Bayfield and most wouldn't see each other until the next sailing season, this event was always well attended. Dr. Art Huderle and O. A. Burghdorf, sailors and gourmets from Duluth, were chefs at these parties for many years. The teenage girls decorated the clubhouse with a different theme each year and helped serve the food. John and Helen Pierpont had the largest family, a daughter and seven sons, but families of four and five children were common among club members. Consequently, the parties were large and boisterous, everybody enjoying the end-of-season festivities.

The attitude toward the rules of sailboat racing among most club members in the early years was casual, perhaps because of the presence of so many children. During one Inter-Island Race, for example, Doc Pierpont, in *Siskiwit*, went aground on the sand off Otter Island. The dozen or so competitors doused their sails and hovered around the helpless vessel. After some discussion, lines were passed between all boats and then finally to the top of *Siskiwit's* mast. With lines everywhere, *Siskiwit* looked as if she had been impaled in a giant spider's web. At a signal, all boats surged forward under power. Quickly, *Siskiwit* was dislodged, lines were hurriedly cast off, and each boat maneuvered to escape her neighbor. The fleet regrouped some distance away from the offending rocks, and at another signal, the race resumed. There were no protests. No one had raced ahead without stopping to help, the winners were valid, and all slept well that night, content that no ill had befallen the fiercely competitive but greatly admired and well liked founder of our sailing club.

A number of races originated in the early golden years of the Apostle Islands Yacht Club: these included the Inter-Island, the Around-the-Islands, the International, and the Trans-Superior races. All are still contested. Members of the club love sailing, love our inland sea, and love life. Our children, now married and with children of their own, say those were the best years of their lives. And Jack ended his sailing days with 41 silver trophies, including three International wins and one Trans-Superior first place win in his class.

Some day a sailor will write a memoir of the Apostle Islands Yacht Club races. He will tell of being in high seas, of one race run in fog so thick not another boat was seen from start to finish. He may remember navigational lights missing in crucial, rock-strewn areas of Canada and the Apostles. But I wish to celebrate the people in the club—particularly John Pierpont, without whom the club surely would not have existed. He is in his seventies now, still racing, still displaying his constant spirited love of sailing, and still extending his welcoming openness to everyone.

Chapter 4

Thunder Bay

In 1970, the Canadian cities of Fort William and Port Arthur became the single city of Thunder Bay. Their 200 years of independent history is deeply rooted in the fur trade. Before the Treaty of Paris of 1783 settled the Revolutionary War between the United States and Great Britain, fur traders had used all harbors on Lake Superior indiscriminately. After the boundary between the United States and British North America was officially determined, however, American fur traders had to stay on the American side of the Pigeon River and the 100-year-old post of Grand Portage became the main fur-trading locale for the American companies (Figures 10–13). The British traders, required to stay north of the Pigeon River, expanded Fort William, a small trading post on the banks of the Kaministikwia River. Prince Arthur's Landing, located at the northern end of the capacious Lakehead Harbor, became the town of Prince Arthur. One hundred eighty seven years later the two communities forsook their original names for a more poetic one.

Figure 10. The Great Hall at the North West Company's post at Grand Portage. This replica was built upon the footings of the original 18th century building. (Jack Soetebier photograph.)

Figure 11. The North West Company's post at Grant Portage, nestled between the shore of Lake superior and the highlands beyond. Visible here are replicas of the Great Hall, the kitchen, and the canoe shed. (Jack Soetebier photograph.)

Figure 12. A 400-year-old witch tree at Grand Portage. Ojibway Indians left offerings to the great Manitou at this site. (Jack Soetebier photograph.)

Figure 13. Spirit houses covering Ojibway graves at Grand Portage Indian Reservation, Minnesota. (Jack Soetebier photograph.)

Father Claude Dablon, the redoubtable Jesuit priest and explorer, wrote in the 1660s that the "great inlet" on Lake Superior bore the name "Thunder" because it was said to thunder there all the time. Another early writer recounted how thunder bounced from one sheer cliff to another. He was referring to the famous landmark, the Sleeping Giant, an 800-foot-high diabase sill, and the neighboring hills which surround Thunder Bay.

A curious description is found in the ancient Chinese book of mountains and seas, the *Shan Hai Jing* (book XIII, translated in 1971 by Cyclone Covey and Dominic Chan). This geography, written in 2000 B.C., tells of two officers sent by their emperor to "pace the limits of the east and west," according to Cyclone Covey in the book *Dragon Treasures*. Covey offers startling and provocative hypotheses and facts to support them. Some scholars, such as Dr. Henriette Mertz, and Wei Chuhsien of Hong Kong University, believe that these early explorers, writing about an area they called Fu Sang, were describing parts of Canada. Fu Sang, the Chinese determined, was 3,300 miles across, east to west, and 3,300 miles from north to south; in one area, "Thunder demons, with bulging dragon bodies and human heads inhabit Thunder Pond in WeSe." Other places described in Fu Sang are "Sweet Lake" and "Floating Ghost Land." Sweet Lake is shaped just like Lake Superior. Could the Floating Ghost Land refer to the northern land under the aurora borealis? The *Shan Hai Jing* remains unsubstantiated, but it is consistent with the discovery of ancient Chinese coins by miners in the soil of British Columbia and of Chinese anchor stones in the waters off the California coast, and it could explain the occurrence of New World peanuts at an archeological site in Chekiange Province in China that is 2,000 years old. After all, those early explorers had to have returned home to make such a detailed report to their emperor.

The Ojibway Indians, residents of the magnificent region around Superior before the European settlers arrived, believed that thunderbirds dwelt in the place we call Thunder Bay. Piles of rock boulders, three feet high and arranged in giant circles four to seven feet across, were found nearby in the Lake Nipigon and central Wisconsin regions. The natives called these rings thunderbird nests. Such rock groupings could very well have been used as solar calendars, as were the monoliths at Stonehenge in Britain and the great circles of wooden posts at Cahokia, Illinois, and Aztalan, Wisconsin, constructed by the mound-building Indians of the Mississippian culture.

On those occasions when the International Race ended in Thunder Bay, our kids and I would take a room high up in the Prince Arthur Hotel from which we watched and waited for our ship to come in. We would stay up all night if the lights of the sailboats were in sight; we would wait a day or two if there was no wind. The kids swam in the hotel pool, and I visited with other waiting supporters. When our boats got in, our crew was always hungry, and after showers for the men, we headed for a restaurant. My favorite one is in the Airlane Motel; the chef, from Switzerland, makes excellent coquilles St. Jacques and other Continental dishes. And there is the Hoito, a modest Finnish eatery within walking distance of the downtown marina, where viili, piirakka, and mojakka have been served since 1918.

Some incidents associated with the races from or into Thunder Bay have become part of our repertoire of Superior stories. One of the racers in 1973 cruised into the harbor at Thunder Bay after midnight for the start of the race the next day. Not wanting to disturb Canadian Customs at such a late hour, the skipper tied up his new sailboat to the Mercantile Dock next to the Prince Arthur Hotel, and he and his crew took a room there for a good night's sleep. Arriving at the dock in the morning, the captain was surprised to see his expensive racing machine guarded by a Royal Canadian Mounted Policeman who declared, "Sir, I have the duty to inform you that this boat is now the property of the Queen."

"You're putting me on!" exclaimed the skipper.

"No, Sir, I'm not" replied the official.

Since the young man had not reported his arrival to Canadian Customs and since he and his crew had left the vessel before being cleared to do so, his craft was impounded by the authorities. A search of the sailboat revealed a handgun, possession of it a severe infraction of Canadian law, and it cost the captain a considerable amount of money in fines and legal fees before his craft was restored to him. We never again saw that fellow in an International Race, but his ex-wife did cruise in the area some years later with a new boat—and a new husband.

Another favorite story of boats and Thunder Bay involves Jean Paul St. Jacques, an Ontario architect who studied at one of Frank Lloyd Wright's ateliers. In the summer of 1968, Jean Paul built his own sailboat, *Pandora's Box*, a sloop constructed of plywood. The International Race began in Thunder Bay that year. The night before the race was to begin, Jean Paul was still drilling holes and putting screws into his masterpiece. The very morning of the race, while the mast was being lowered into its step, the crew was scurrying around installing all of the lines for the rigging. Twenty minutes after the official start of the Third International Sailboat Race, *Pandora's Box* crossed the starting line, sails raised for the first time. Her rigging was completed during the course of her shakedown cruise, the 140-mile race across Lake Superior to Bayfield! She came in last—under full sail—to the cheers of the crowd.

Thunder Bay is now a second home to us. We have many friends there, and we visit often by boat and car.

Old Fort William, a reconstruction of the 18th century fur post located on the western edge of modern Thunder Bay, is a wonderful attraction and I never tire of viewing it (Figures 14 and 15). There is no more truthful representation of the life of the colorful French voyageurs who preceded us on the waters and shores of the great lake in the 17th and 18th centuries. Those hardy sailors rowed 40-foot Montreal canoes made of birchbark and pine tree pitch from Montreal to Grand Portage every summer (Figure 16). They exchanged the iron axes, kettles and guns, blankets and beads, and tobacco they had carried so far for the furs that the native Ojibway had trapped throughout the winter, and then returned to Montreal. We follow in their wake yearly in a comfortable boat, fueled by gasoline-powered engines, with electric stove, refrigerator, and heater. They transported four ton per canoe with only their strong arms and hands as their source of power, with

Figure 14. The Great Hall of the North West Company's post as reconstructed at Old Fort William. (Jack Soetebier photograph.)

Figure 15. Birchbark wigwam in the Ojibway encampment as reconstructed at Old Fort William. (Jack Soetebier photograph.)

Figure 16. A 36-foot-long Montreal canoe. These canoes each carried three-and-one-half ton of trade goods from Montreal to Grand Portage and Fort William. (Jack Soetebier photograph.)

perhaps the assistance of a little wind at their backs now and then. They slept beneath overturned canoes at night on the rocky beaches of the lake and sustained themselves daily on dried pea soup and hardtack bread. My admiration for them is unbounded.

Fort William, however, commemorates the more comfortable lifestyle the voyageurs enjoyed during the great exchange of goods. For a week or two, a voyageur slept in a bunkhouse, ate fresh vegetables and raised bread fresh from an outdoor oven, and renewed his supply of tobacco, pipes, and rum from the storekeeper (Figure 17). He rested his body for the return trip, revitalized his soul with singing and dancing to the fiddle, and exchanged tall tales with members of other brigades waiting at the fort as was he.

The Fort William of today is much larger than the original fort. By 1803, the beaver felt hat was no longer the fashion in Europe, and the tremendous demand for the pelts of the hardy animal had diminished. Fort William was used as a trading post for only 20 years, then it fell into disuse and disrepair.

Old Fort William is a handsome structure comprising 40 buildings and a wharf on the river. It was built according to the long range plans for the original post, but it is not located on the original site, as is Grand Portage National Monument nearby in Minnesota. Still, the life of the mid-18th century has been captured accurately—the farmers use horses to draw their plows, the milkmaid milks the dairy cows by hand and then turns the cream into butter by hand-churning. Within the picket post walls, a cooper, a tinsmith, and other craftsmen ply their trades. One can visualize the partners of the North West Company meeting and making decisions about their thriving business (Figure 18). But best of all, in the canoe shed, workers build North and Montreal canoes—they shape the frame and ribs, and then cover this skeleton with large pieces of birch bark glued together with hot pine pitch (Figures 19 and 20). The voyageur was a brave man, indeed, to venture onto a great body of water in such a fragile craft!

The authenticity of Old Fort William is amply attested to by a friend who was chosen to oversee the construction of the 65-foot sail ship there as an exhibit. He had built his own yawl in timely fashion, so we inquired why it was taking five years to build the wooden boat at Old Fort William.

"First we have to wait for a beaver to chew down a mast for us!" he said.

Figure 17. An outdoor bread oven at Old Fort William. (Jack Soetebier photograph.)

Figure 18. Interior of the Great Hall at Old Fort William. Here, partners of the North West Company dined well in the wilderness during the annual rendezvous in August. (Jack Soetebier photograph.)

Figure 19. Outside the canoe shed, Old Fort William. Cedar ribs were steamed in wooden boxes prior to being bent and fitted onto canoe frames, and pitch and ash for use in sealing patches of birch bark were heated in kettles. (Jack Soetebier photograph.)

Figure 20. Inside the canoe shed, Old Fort William, showing North canoes. Smaller than Montreal canoes, North canoes were used for river travel. (Jack Soetebier photograph.)

Chapter 5

Silver Islet

There lies no more romantic spot on the shores of Lake Superior than Silver Islet.

Twenty miles east of Thunder Bay, directly behind the rocky foot of the Sleeping Giant, lies Silver Islet—a small settlement well known in the financial circles of England, Scotland, Ireland, and the United States throughout the 1870s as Silver Islet Landing (Figure 21). What was at that time the richest silver ore in the world, assayed at between 2.76 percent and 5.50 percent silver, had been discovered in 1868 half a mile offshore on 90-foot-long Skull Rock. Soon thereafter, Silver Islet Mine was established on Skull Rock—it the Silver Islet for which the settlement was named (Figures 22 and 23).

The mine could not have been built had it not been for the most extraordinarily creative Irish-born engineer, William Bell Frue. Frue, who had had extensive experience in the copper mines of Michigan's Upper Peninsula, arrived at Silver Islet on September 1, 1870, with a boatload of Cornish miners. He had them construct a 460-foot breakwater crib and a cofferdam within

Figure 21. Silver Islet Landing—miners' homes on the Ontario mainland. The Jules Cross-James Crooks house is that nearest the viewer. (From *Canadian Geographical Journal*, 87(2).)

Figure 22. Silver Islet Mine, 1921. (From *Canadian Geographical Journal*, 87(2).)

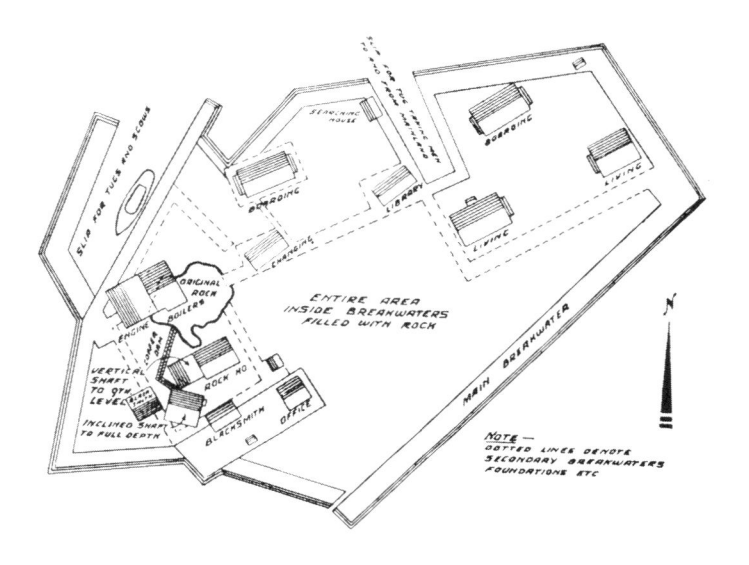

Figure 23. Plan of Silver Islet Mine, 1882. (From *Canadian Geographical Journal*, 87(2).)

the breakwater to enclose the rich ore vein. The cofferdam was pumped day and night, and by October 5, 1870, silver was being extracted through a shaft in Skull Rock only a few feet above the surface of the lake.

Four major storms struck the Silver Islet area during the fall and winter of 1870–71. The cofferdam remained firm, but the breakwater and its 6,000 ton of rock and 50,000 feet of timber spilled out into the lake with each renewed blast.

Frue, not one to concede victory to the lake, began rebuilding the breakwater early in the spring. He employed 480 men to build a four-acre crib surrounding the bald rock. The space around the shaft was filled with stones and cement, and the mine thus was converted to a profitable underground operation. After two years of production, the Silver Islet Mine had shipped three-quarters of a million dollars in silver across the unpredictable waters of Lake Superior to Detroit, Toronto, and Montreal, and the value of the mining stock climbed from $50 per share to $25,000. The mine was in operation only 13 years, but a total of $3,250,000 worth of silver had been extracted from the mine on tiny Skull Rock.

In 1873, Frue invented a device which is still in use in mining today, the Frue Vanner. It consisted of an India rubber belt mounted on rollers which shook rapidly from side to side. Crushed rock was carried along the belt; a water spray washed the lighter particles of rock away, allowing the heavier silver to travel into a container at the end. The manufacture and distribution of the vanner absorbed Frue; in 1874, he filed Canada Patent #3974, and in July 1875, he resigned his position at Silver Islet Mine. He died at his home in Detroit in 1881.

Meanwhile, at Silver Islet Landing on the mainland, a thriving community of 300 souls had built 50 homes, a general store, a school, two churches, a boarding house, and a jail. A combined library–tavern allowed a workman to drink but three glasses of liquor in any 24-hour period. The mine president's house boasted 21 rooms, a grand piano among its furnishings, and negro servants to attend to the Victoria coach and drive the horses (Figure 24).

English lords and ladies, artists, professors, senators, and bishops were among the visitors to Silver Islet in those early years, and the mining community produced at least one princess. Eber B. Ward of Detroit was one of the largest stockholders of the Silver Islet Mine. His daughter Clara became, upon her marriage, the Princess of Chimay and lived near Stratford-on-Avon in Charlecote Park—one of England's great homes, even to this day. Clara died in Padua, Italy.

Figure 24. Homes and boats of the fishing Finns at the east end of Silver Islet Harbor. The mine president's home stood here in the 1870s. (Jack Soetebier photograph.)

In February of 1884, the silver in the mine and the steam that worked the pumps removing Superior's icy waters from the shafts gave out simultaneously, and the mine has not been worked seriously since. The miners and their families left the way they had arrived, by boat, with as many of their household goods as possible, and simply resigned their homes to the elements and the wild animals. At the turn of the century, families from Port Arthur and Fort William began sailing out for the summer months, adopting the homes which had best withstood the weathering of the intervening years.

The first time that we saw Silver Islet, we were cruising in John Pierpont's *Siskiwit* (Figure 25). Jack had skippered the craft in the International Sailboat Race in John's absence, and we were returning *Siskiwit* to her home port of Bayfield by way of Thunder Bay. The

Figure 25. Silver Islet today, the island where the world's richest silver mine was located in the 1870s. (Bill MacDonald photograph.)

houses of the fabled village looked as they must have 100 years before—the wooden log and frame buildings, weathered and gray instead of white-washed, crouched before the steep, shaly cliffs along an avenue, flowers blooming brightly in each yard, and thunderous waves lashing at their feet. Some of the houses had the original wallpaper and well-worn furniture. Without modern plumbing and electricity, the village is now a kind of living museum. We wanted to see the mine island, so Ron Thomson took us there by outboard motorboat. Nothing of the mine remained to be seen but a bit of a wall of some sort protruding above the weeds and stunted trees. Even with the deterioration, however, both the island and the ghost of the former community on the shore are magical to me.

The second time we tied up to the stout dock at Silver Islet—as the community on the shore has been known since the early 1900s—we were aboard our own *Blitzen*. Mabel Crooks came down from the avenue and visited us. When I said that I had been in several of the old houses and had decided that I wasn't going to die until I had seen every one of them, Mabel said, "I'll tell you how to get into one of the most historic of all. It has lots of items and wallpaper from the mining days. It's the Matthews house. You knock at the door tomorrow at 10 in the morning and say that your grandfather, whose name was Stevens, was the mine captain here back in the 1880s. Say that he used to live in the house, and that you would like to see it. And then I'll come and introduce you to the present owner."

That sounded good enough to me. The next morning, as I prepared to walk up to the mine captain's house, our crew member that summer—Pat Stevens—said, "You're not going through with this, are you?"

"Why not," said I. "Come along."

"Nothing doing. Mabel wasn't serious."

So, Pat stayed aboard *Blitzen* with her husband Steve and Jack. I trotted up to the house alone.

My knock at the well-weathered front door brought a very pregnant, beautiful blond woman in her early 40s to open it. I repeated Mabel's words about my grandfather, the mine captain, and wanting to see where he had lived. The woman made no move to let me enter, so I prattled on for some minutes, making up a more and more fantastic story as I went along, all the while looking up and down the avenue for the one who had put me up to this. At last, I confessed that Mabel Crooks had suggested this and that she was supposed to have met me here at 10:00 A.M.

"Oh, Mabel!" exclaimed the woman and, opening the door wide, invited me in. She was having a coffee klatch with several friends, but she herself was drinking beer because she was having a hot flash—Larry Matthews was pregnant with a change-of-life baby. This was my first experience with Mabel's practical jokes. She never did come to the Matthews' house that morning!

Unbeknownst to me, two strangers had come to Larry's door that summer already with the same story about Stevens, the mine captain, as a means of seeing her historic house. We'll never know if Mabel Crooks put them all up to it. What we do know, however, is that when I didn't return to *Blitzen*, Pat—our crew member—walked up to the Matthews' house and knocked on the door. When Larry answered, Pat said "I'm Pat Stevens . . . ."

Larry cried, "Oh, come on in!"

Pat and I had a great visit with Larry and her friends, and we had a tour of what is perhaps the best preserved historic home in Silver Islet. Best of all, however, we became friends with Larry and enjoyed this relationship until her untimely death some years later.

One of the largest houses in Silver Islet belonged for many years to Jules Cross, a noted spiritualist. Supposedly, Mr. Booker, the last person buried in the Silver Islet cemetery, could be summoned from time to time by table tapping, both in his home and in some of the other older buildings. So well known were the spirits around Silver Islet that the Metaphysical Society of North America held its annual convention at Jules's house during the summer of 1934. The participants arrived by boat, most of them clad in black, according to an eye witness. As they walked along the avenue en route to the Cross home, they looked for all the world like the cast of the television comedy series *The Munsters*. There is no record to tell whether Mr. Booker did or did not attend the international seance.

Some 40 years after the Metaphysical Society met at Silver Islet, Mabel and Jamie Crooks bought the Jules Cross home (Figure 21). They immediately brought two friends out to see their purchase. It was early in winter; all the camps, except for the fishing Finns, were closed and sealed up against the winter winds. After a tour of the building, Jamie busied himself starting a fire in the wood stove in the kitchen, while Mabel got out the picnic lunch. As the foursome began eating, some low moans could be heard. Mabel, who knew the ghostly background of this particular house, was instantly alarmed, but as the guests appeared not to have heard anything, she hoped it was just the sound of wind in an old house. But, no! The sounds became more and more pronounced, and Mabel was weighing in her mind the reputation of Jules' home and the substantial sum of money they had just paid for it, when suddenly a telephone rang! Silver Islet has no such modern conveniences, but the practical jokers had forgotten about that when making the tape of moans and groans. They had placed a tape player next to a grating through which the heat from the wood stove rose in the old days to warm the bedrooms above, and during the tour of the house they had activated the tape. This is the best practical joke ever played on Mabel, herself a champion of the genre.

I have been visiting Silver Islet for 27 years now, and I've seen about half of the historic homes in the settlement. We've gone to this place at least once each year: with our children, with friends who have never heard of it, for Canadian Thanksgiving, and for parties. The saunas, the practical jokes, the sheer beauty of the place are deeply and extensively entwined with the lives of our family. The closest to a mystical experience we ever had there occurred in 1981. Our friend Sally Meyer had died in May of that year, of leukemia. Sally often had wished to visit Silver Islet, but life had taken her to Seattle instead. At her tender funeral, the choir sang *Amazing Grace*. That summer at the dock at Silver Islet we met a Canadian who had sailed from North Bay on Lake Huron across Lake Superior on a 25-foot boat—with his bagpipes. He sat up with us through a tornado watch one night until 2:00 A.M., entertaining us with the marvelous sound of his instrument. When the watch was finally cancelled, he walked back to his boat, in the darkness, playing one last song for us—*Amazing Grace*. I felt at that moment that Sally finally had made it to Silver Islet.

Chapter 6

Otter Cove

Over the years, either to spend the night or to escape bad weather, we have anchored in many little coves along the North Shore of Lake Superior. Each is unique. Only a few between Silver Islet and the little village of Rossport have docks. Dr. Buddy Saunders of Thunder Bay has a private dock in Walker's Channel, but it is a very difficult place to navigate into because the waterway is narrow and a rocky shoal lies right in the middle of it. On Porphyry Island, behind the lighthouse, there is a substantial dock that is used often by vessels of the Canadian Coast Guard when they are working in the area. The channel leading to this dock is dog-legged in shape, but the location does offer good protection from nearly all winds. Many coves have delighted us with their wildlife. Loon Harbor to the east has sheltered our various boats many a time, and, although we've often seen pairs of loons around the lake, it was there that we witnessed a flock of loons, all chortling and crooning together, calling and answering each other. Otter Cove,

Figure 26. Showering at Otter Cove Waterfall. (Jack Soetebier photograph.)

however, is the best place we know along this part of the coast for observing wildlife.

Otter Cove is an arm of water that snakes deep into the land and ends at a waterfall (Figure 26). The river that enters Otter Cove, formerly used as a logging flume, cascades 50 feet down a cliff to algae- and moss-covered boulders below. Around the base of this waterfall is a reedy marsh, and in the hills above it are skeletons of ancient pine trees. All of this provides the backdrop to a wild animal paradise.

In the mud bank at the far end of the cove lives the biggest, fattest beaver I have ever seen. He minces out of his hideout from time to time into the sunlight. The waters seem to be good pike habitat, and osprey fish here constantly. And a pair of bald eagles have a nest in a needleless pine at the entrance to the cove; in the summer, the huge castle of dry, whitened branches shelters little bobbing heads. Aboard our boat at quiet anchor, we have watched one of the adult eagles hunt in majestic figure-eights in the sky. There are always families of mallards and, of course, gulls. At least one heron returns each year to this avian cornucopia. On one visit, we watched an adolescent heron for an hour. Partly hidden in the bushes, his brilliant white breast plumage gave him away, for it sparkled in the sunlight every time he turned his head, elegant with its sharp black feathers and eyes. We once saw a skunk swimming across the cove, an observation not many people believe except that Jack captured the event on video tape. But best of all, in 1988, for the first time, we observed the beautiful creatures for whom the place was named—the river otters. A small family gamboled and played in the still waters, moving up and down so rapidly that the troupe of four looked for all the world like a sea dragon, undulating over the surface of the water. This sight was simply beautiful!

We anchored the *Dutchman* in Otter Cove one fine day in July of 1989. Enjoying the company of sailors from other craft anchored in the cove, we were playing some classical music of the Galant era. The harpsichord, flutes, and violins twinkled and trilled; suddenly, a goldfinch in the woods close by began to answer and repeat the music whenever there was a lull in the tape. This went on for 20 or 30 minutes, and we were delighted that a wild bird would respond so enthusiastically to our canned music.

The next morning, no sounds were to be heard in this protected harbor where six sailboats and one powerboat were anchored. Crews were taking advantage of their holidays to sleep in. Suddenly, from the same nearby woods where the bird had been singing the previous evening, there now came the same trills and cadenzas which had previously accompanied Hayden. We didn't turn on our tape player to answer the singing bird in deference to our drowsy neighbors. The bird, however, sang furiously, paused and sang again, just as he had the night before. After 20 minutes or so of fruitless calling to the harpsichord, the flute, and the violin, he ceased his beautiful song and departed.

We'll remember the responsive songbird on our next visit to Otter Cove. The heron and eagle come back year after year, so perhaps the songster also will return another year for a second boffo duet with our classical music.

Chapter 7

Rossport and Nipigon

Our vacation cruise of 1975 took Jack and I, and our daughters Gretchen and Heidi, then 16 and eight years old, to Rossport, Ontario, on Superior's North Shore. We first sailed to the Slate Islands, rocky islands in the northernmost part of Lake Superior boasting herds of wild caribou and virgin trout—fish that have not been planted by some governmental agency. However, we saw neither during our stay. From the Slate Islands, we sailed up Simpson Channel to picturesque Rossport, a fishing village ringed by a towering pink cuesta that is topped by magnificent dark evergreens.

We approached the public dock at dusk, and we could see scores of people crowding it and the adjacent shoreline. I thought to myself, "This is such a small, remote town that the entire population has come down to see our sailboat. We're probably the only visitors they have had all month!"

Wrong! As we approached, not a soul left the crowd to so much as catch our dock lines. Instead they were hypnotized by a strange little contraption in the water close to shore. It was a prototype of a submersible!

One mile or so from Rossport lay the McGarvey Shoals, a barely submerged pinnacle of rock surrounded on all sides by cold, clear Lake Superior water 250 feet deep. This rock, a considerable hazard to navigation, has been marked by buoys many times over the years, but the fury of the lake, its currents, and the ice, have dislodged most of them. In 1980, scuba divers found five buoys and their anchors resting on a shelf of the vertical face of this underwater cliff at a depth of 90 feet.

Apparently nothing marked the dangerous shoals in the summer of 1911, when the touring luxury yacht, the *Gunilda*, built in Scotland of steel, ran into them while under a full head of steam (Figure 27). Her owner, William Harkness, the heir to the Standard Oil Company, was aboard with a party. Her captain, unfamiliar with the details of the Lake Superior shoreline, had advised Mr. Harkness to hire a local pilot, but the sum of $25 had seemed too large to the millionaire. Instead, a salvage company tug boat from Port Arthur had to be engaged, at a considerably higher fee, in an attempt to pull the vessel free, but her stern filled with water and she sank on the spot.

The timing of our arrival at Rossport was perfect—the submersible being tested in the harbor was destined to explore the *Gunilda*. A consortium of scuba divers from Rochester, Michigan, had just built the small, two-man submarine and had transported it by flatbed trailer to Rossport with the express intention of finding the *Gunilda*. This was to be the little vessel's sea trial. As we tied *Hussar* at the town dock, the submersible's crew was in the process of testing all machine systems prior to the first deep dive. The crew hired a local fisherman who towed the submersible out to McGarvey Shoals in the morning. They hoped to be there before the wind

Figure 27. The yacht *Gunilda*, the "Reluctant Lady," on McGarvey Shoals off Rossport. (From photograph in collection of Edmund L. Basher.)

came up, because the craft was unstable on the surface. Two members of the team submerged and actually located the *Gunilda*. The next morning we had breakfast with the crew, and they raved about the beauty of the yacht. The name could be seen plainly, they said, the gold leaf still bright despite so many years in the depths; the woodwork and rigging were all splendidly preserved. The Jacques Cousteau team explored the *Gunilda* in 1984 and pronounced her the most perfectly preserved sunken ship they had ever seen.

 The lives of two scuba divers have been lost on dives to the *Gunilda*: one in August, 1970, and another in August, 1989. Despite the difficulties of reaching the *Gunilda*, divers still are lured to her because she is so perfectly preserved. The top section of the ship's mast had been removed in 1965, the navigation light still operational. It is now installed outside the Rossport Inn as a memorial to the ship itself and the two divers who died exploring her.

Figure 28. The 100-year-old Rossport Inn. (From postcard in collection of Edmund L. Basher.)

The two-story frame Rossport Inn was built more than 100 years ago next to the Canadian Pacific railway tracks. It served as depot and hotel combined, as did a string of such buildings across Canada at the turn of the century. In 1971, Jack and crewman Ned Basher, a jet pilot in the United States Air Force, had sailed to Rossport on their way to Sault Ste. Marie, Michigan, for the second Trans-Superior Sailboat Race. Ned was attracted to the historic hotel, and in 1982, he purchased it (Figure 28). He has remodeled and restored it, transforming it into a successful bed and breakfast inn which boasts a sauna near an icy trout stream. Six bedrooms sport Hudson Bay blankets on the beds, and the restaurant serves gourmet dinners, featuring local trout.

Ned opens the Rossport Inn each year early in May and closes it in November at the end of moose hunting season in Ontario. Geologists and officials of the nearby Hemlo gold mine are regulars, and tourists find their way from the nearby Trans-Canada Highway. Ned works from dawn to dark in the busy summer season, and travels south during the winter for rest and relaxation.

Several winters ago Ned met a tall, beautiful Canadian named Shelagh in a commuter airport in the Bahamas. He didn't remember her last name, but he did recall that she worked in a health club in Winnipeg. She stayed in his mind, and upon his return to Rossport, he telephoned friends in Winnipeg and set them to searching for the fascinating Shelagh. There are a hundred health clubs in Winnipeg; the friends dutifully began calling them, asking for an employee named Shelagh.

In the meantime, Shelagh remembered Ned too. When her parents decided to drive from Winnipeg to Toronto in the spring that followed, Shelagh suggested that they stop at the Rossport Inn on their way by. They did. Ned now had the last name of the young woman, and her address! He sent her a dozen roses and a one-way train ticket to Rossport. Her parents would be returning in a week or so, he wrote; she could visit him and then go home with her parents on their way back. Shelagh took the train to the front door of the Rossport Inn—and has never left!

Shelagh and Ned married in 1986. Her improvements to the Inn include smoked lake trout, fresh homemade breads and pies, blueberry preserves, and decorated birthday cakes and tortes. Our stop at the Rossport Inn is always a highlight of our trip.

For many years Jack and I have been celebrating Canadian Thanksgiving, which occurs on the second weekend of October, with our friends at Silver Islet. In 1988, we visited Ned and Shelagh, but this time in the fall as part of our Canadian Thanksgiving trip, and we arrived at Rossport in time to witness what I expect is a once-in-a-lifetime scene. Oil tanks were docked at Rossport harbor!

Two giant oil tanks were being towed from the Thunder Bay waterfront to Lake Erie, the tugboat skippered by Fred Broennele. In the heavy weather common on Lake Superior at this time of the year, one of the tanks broke loose and ran aground in Armour Harbor 15 miles southwest of Rossport. Fred towed the tank that was still attached to his towline into Rossport's harbor and anchored it on the waterfront, then he and Ned returned in the tug for the stray tank. They had some difficulty securing the recalcitrant tank, but they did succeed in pulling it off the beach and towing it right into downtown Rossport where tug and tank tied up at the main town dock. We awoke in the inn to look out our window and see the Broennele's tug fire up her engines and slowly steam out of the harbor, rather majestically I thought, with a huge circular tank serenely following along behind. We were later told that the tug and its tow sat out some gusty 50-mile-an-hour winds in various small harbors along Superior's coast, but the tug eventually delivered the tank safely to its destination. The second tank was returned the following year to Thunder Bay where it was scrapped.

Forty miles or so from Rossport, the little community of Nipigon sits on the shore at the mouth of a river bearing the same name. The Nipigon River connects the Nipigon Straits to Lake Nipigon, the lake well known for its excellent fishing and long-used by voyageurs to reach the fur-rich area beyond (Figures 29 and 30). In August, 1919, Edward, Prince of Wales, visited Lake Nipigon, where he fished and paddled a canoe in a fedora. While there, he was installed as a member of the local Ojibway band and given the name Chief Morning Star. Surely, his party of 58 people in 22 canoes was the largest fishing party ever on this renowned lake. Maybe Prince Edward also saw the pictographs near the town.

Figure 29. Prince Edward, the Prince of Wales, and members of his party canoeing on Lake Nipigon in 1919. (From *The Jewels of the Duchess of Windsor*, The Vendome Press.)

Figure 30. Prince Edward—Chief Morning Star of the Ojibway. (From *The Jewels of the Duchess of Windsor*, The Vendome Press.)

One half mile away from and opposite the townsite of Nipigon, a high cliff towers straight up above the waters of the Nipigon River (Figure 31). Although the rock itself is fairly light in color, it is streaked by red minerals seeping through crevices and by red lichen clinging to the sheer face of the cliff. A pictograph in red is clearly visible—a stylized human figure and a shape resembling a canoe with sticks in it. The artist probably pulverized hematite and mixed it with glue-like material from fish to paint the pictures on the rock. The paintings existed in this spot when the earliest explorers and voyageurs appeared in the region, and to this day, Native Americans leave gifts of tobacco and red ribbons at this place.

I have also seen the pictographs at Agawa on the eastern side of Lake Superior (Figures 32 and 33). To get to them, one walks down a steep rocky slope between two immense, straight, vertical rock cuts, like being between two very tall and dark skyscrapers. This is a fault line—the trace of an ages old fracture in the rock, as straight and even as if cut by a sharp knife. Water oozes through crevices in the rock and moistens the path. Suddenly, one comes upon hundreds of boulders, of all sizes, thrown this way and that, all having tumbled one after the other down still farther to the lake shore. It looks as if a giant baby, in a fit of bad temper, scattered his toy building blocks all about. Most of the rocks are gray, salt-and-pepper granite, but beneath the water, at the edge of the cliff, there are huge white boulders gleaming menacingly despite the waves. The ancient pictographs on the face of the cliff overlook the open waters of the lake; they illustrate the great horned serpent Misshepezhieu, various other serpents, and a canoe—powerful medicine!

These are the only pictographs I have seen on Lake Superior. Both are located on rock faces associated with

Figure 31. The Nipigon pictographs. Top: The rock face upon which the pictographs are located, at tip of arrow. Bottom: Tracing of part of the pictographs. The squatting man figure is a Maymaygwayshi, a naughty little water man. (Jack Soetebier photograph; tracing from *Indian Rock Paintings of the Great Lakes*, University of Toronto Press.)

Figure 32. The Agawa pictographs site. (From *Indian Rock Paintings of the Great Lakes*, University of Toronto Press; original published in *The Telegram*, Toronto.)

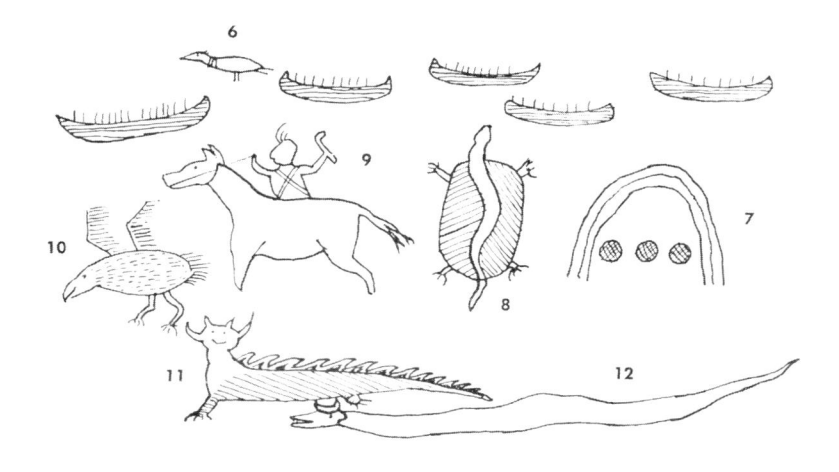

Figure 33. The Agawa pictographs. Top: Renditions of the pictographs by Henry Rowe Schoolcraft, based on an informants recollections as recorded on birch bark. (From *Indian Rock Paintings of the Great Lakes*, University of Toronto Press.) Bottom: Rock face showing pictograph. (Paul Hayden/*Lake Superior Magazine* photograph.)

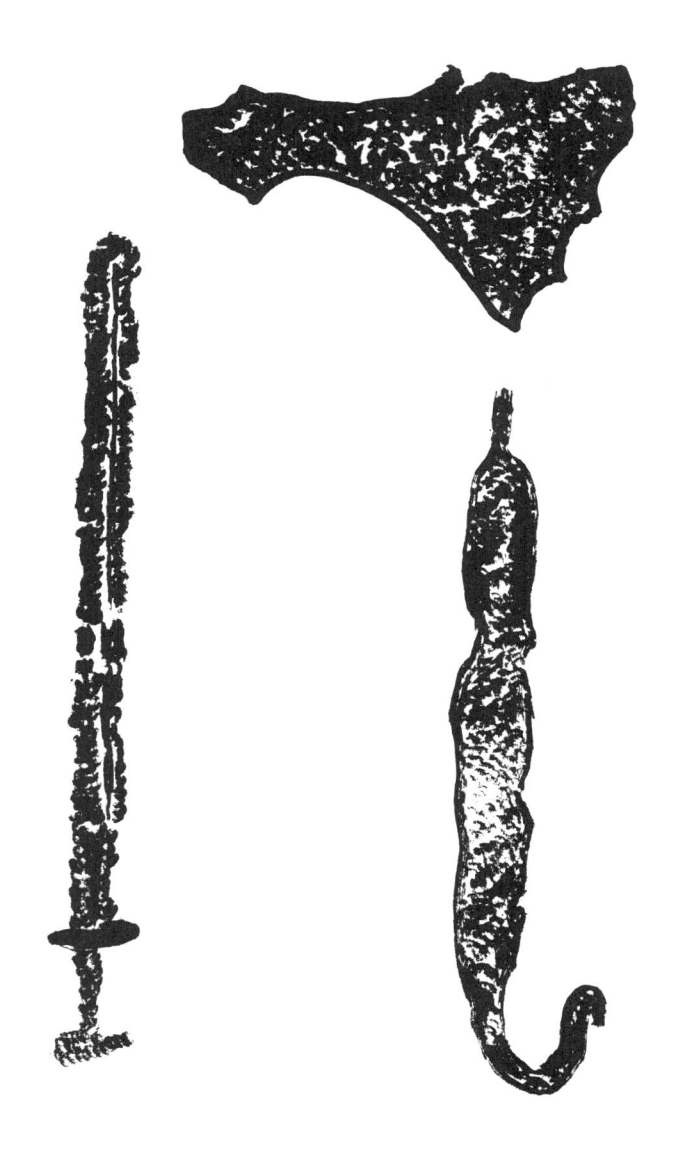

Figure 34. The Beardmore Relics in the Royal Ontario Museum, Toronto. Left: The 30-inch corroded sword. Top: the wrought-iron axehead. Bottom: Possibly a Viking *rangel*. The relics are not shown at the same scale. (Drawings by the author.)

fault lines on the lake. The Ojibway believed that Misshepezhieu, the great horned spirit, governed the waters of the lake; it stands to reason, therefore, that they would believe that areas where great movements of the earth had obviously taken place must have had some connection with that powerful entity. Around Lake Superior where one rocky nook and magnificent mountain is more beautiful than the next, it is certain that both Agawa and Nipigon Straits stand out.

The small Nipigon Museum, which burned down in 1990, had copies of the interesting Beardmore relics on display (Figure 34). While prospecting for gold in 1913, James Dodd of Port Arthur claimed to have discovered some rusty pieces of iron adjacent to an exposed vertical vein of quartz near Beardmore. His story was discredited by a friend who claimed to have seen the items in Dodd's basement earlier. Nonetheless, all the objects are made of iron: the sword is Norse, a style common 900 to 1,000 years ago; the axehead is Norwegian and slightly younger than the sword; and the third piece is thought to be a *rangel*, an object often found in Viking graves. How did the Beardmore relics come to be on the shores of Lake Superior, whether at Beardmore or Port Arthur? Had Vikings traveled this far inland? It was certainly possible for them, given their boating and sailing skills. Or had the items been carried to Canada by a Scandinavian immigrant, as some people contend? Or is there some other explanation? Perhaps the truth will never be determined.

Chapter 8

Isle Royale

Isle Royale—crumbly cake of sedimentary rock infiltrated by lava flows and chock full of copper deposits, scoured and polished by ancient glaciers into dramatic, slanted, rocky outcrops (Figure 2). Isle Royale—an island of mystery and awe for centuries to natives of the Superior shores and now to newcomers too. Ingeborg Holte (Figure 35), who lived some 80 summers on the island, wrote in *Ingeborg's Isle Royale*, ". . . the incomparable Island. The creator molded it with a Master's hand. . . . The archipelago consists of over 200 islands surrounding Isle Royale and many more located in the inland lakes. There are so many fine harbors and bays . . . ."

The Ojibway revealed stories and superstitions about the island and its fabled copper to early European explorers and missionaries. Father Allouez described how the Ojibway prized copper pieces as gifts of the gods, who dwelt beneath the water, and upon which their welfare depended. Father Dablon claimed to have considerable knowledge of four Indians who had landed

Figure 35. Ingeborge Holte on cabin porch, welcoming the author to Wright Island, 1970s. (Tom Haas photograph.)

on a floating island, which was almost always surrounded by fog. The Indians heated their meal by throwing red-hot stones, found on the shore, from their fire into a bark dish, filled with water. They took some of the copper stones and slabs they had found on the island away with them when they departed. Soon a powerful voice called to them, "Who are those robbers carrying off from me my children's cradles and playthings?" So terrorized were the travellers that one died before reaching the mainland, and after relating their tale, the others also died. Louis Denis, Sieur de la Ronde, was warned of "a floating island of copper which no mortal could approach for it was guarded by spirits who could strike all intruders dead."

When white settlers began mining copper on Isle Royale in 1843, they were amazed to discover many prehistoric mines. In 1870, a mining expert estimated that there were 3,000 copper pits on the island and 1,000 ton of the stone hammers that were the main tools of the native miners. Many of the original mines were deep, some as much as 60 feet, although most were 10 to 12 feet deep; and most were 10 to 30 feet in diameter. In 1875, A. C. Davis, superintendent of the Minong Company at McCargoe's Cove, reported to the Smithsonian Institution on the techniques used by the Indian miners. He wrote that, upon opening a transverse vein on the property, he found that ". . . the ancient miner had used large granite boulders to hold up the hanging ground. These boulders would weigh from 300 to 400 pounds, and were put in where the modern miner would place timber, to secure the ground. Nearly all of the brands and timber we found in the pits were roots and stumps. This with the fact of their using these large stones for timber, leads me to think that the ancient miners had used up all the timber in their reach and consequently could not prosecute mining further."

It was shown in the 1950s just how old a tradition mining was on Isle Royale. A radiocarbon date obtained on a charred log found in one pit showed that the log had been burned 3,800 ± 500 years ago.

The copper occurred in large masses called float copper. These masses could be huge. For example, during the summer of 1878, a mass of copper that weighed six ton, was removed from the Minong Mine. Although it had not been worked by the prehistoric miners, one drift had run within two feet of it. The ancient miners worked the copper by heating the huge masses and breaking off manageable pieces. In 1879, several large, previously worked nuggets were discovered in the Minong Mine: one weighed 3,317 pounds, another weighed 4,174 pounds. It is puzzling that graves have not been found on Isle Royale. This suggests that there were no permanent settlements on Isle Royale. The copper workers were probably commuters, despite the fact that the island is 20 miles from the Canadian shore and 50 miles from Michigan's Upper Peninsula! And the mining operations would have required many workers. It has been estimated that it would take 10,000 men, using the type of simple tools found on the sites, working for 1,000 years to remove as much copper as appears to have been removed from the pits.

Copper from Isle Royale, as well as from the Keweenaw Peninsula to the south—essentially the same copper crops out in both areas, the Isle Royale copper more frequently occurring in large nuggets, the Keweenaw in sheets—contains particles of silver large enough to be visible to the naked eye. Archeologists have discovered copper artifacts, such as jewelry and plates, made of native copper containing silver particles, in graves throughout the midwestern United States. More tantalizing is the fact that objects of native copper containing silver also have been excavated in Mexico and Egypt. Did some of these grave goods or the copper from which they are made originate on Isle Royale? It is now theoretically possible to answer this question because Dr. George Rapp, of the University of Minnesota-Duluth, has perfected a method of "finger-printing" native metals which can be used to determine their geographic point of origin. Maybe a tiny piece of an artifact can be sacrificed to science and the chemical fingerprint determined.

Isle Royale never fails to beckon us. The destination of our first boat excursion on Lake Superior, this island became an annual destination on our boating vacations. Once, cruising in the company of Jamie Crooks and family, we tied their sloop *Bara* and our *Hussar* to the Moskey Basin dock. It was such a hot day, the men in the group and Gretchen took turns running along the cement dock, holding onto our main halyard, swinging out over the water, and letting go to drop into the cool lake waters. After a picnic supper, we shared a spirited game of Monopoly to finish the day. That was a typical cruising day with our family and friends.

Since 1931, Isle Royale has been a national park—the foxes are irritatingly tame; the moose, though reticent, are almost always in evidence; but the famous wolves are rarely seen by visitors. Wildlife can always be enjoyed here, especially a plentitude of birds: loons, ducks, and gulls. And near the rocky reefs that surround the island, trout and salmon abound.

The wild blueberries are always ripe when we are on the island, so we have a fresh pie at least once each trip. On one occasion, our friend Ned Basher, six-year-old Heidi, and I climbed the rounded rocky hills above Chippewa Harbor and picked wild blueberries among the low, gray, dry, and springy reindeer moss. As we returned to the boat several hours later, buckets filled, we smelled fresh bread baking. Instead of napping as he had intended, Jack had spent the time making sourdough bread in the oven of our little gimballed boat stove. For dinner that night we feasted on berries and milk with fresh bread and butter. I've never had a better meal.

We fished off Isle Royale often. Trolling slowly, we'd net a coho salmon or lake trout, usually both. Over the

Figure 36. The steamer *America* during her working days. (Lake Superior Marine Museum photograph.)

Figure 37. The *America* on shoals at Isle Royale. (Lake Superior Marine Museum photograph.)

years we have seen the devastating effects of the sea lamprey, a stowaway on ocean vessels entering the St. Lawrence Seaway, on the lake trout population. A parasite, the lamprey attaches itself to the trout by means of a suction mouth and actually sucks the life blood from the fish. Departments of Natural Resources have been poisoning the sea lamprey in the tributary streams of the great lakes where it lives during the early stages of its development, and it is now somewhat in check. As a result, the lake trout population has increased especially around Royale's rocky reefs, and it seems to be healthier. It was not uncommon 25 years ago to see a large trout with three or more lamprey marks on every part of its body. The fish we are catching now are of good size yet bear fewer marks, some only one mark.

The wreck of the *America,* a 937-ton steel coastal steamer that went down off Washington Harbor, is well known because the waters are a prime fishing area (Figures 36 and 37). There are still some Duluthians who remember well the night of June 7, 1928, and they have interesting stories to tell. The 183-foot passenger and freight ship struck a pinnacle rock at 3:00 A.M. and sank in 100 feet of water, but no lives were lost. Her bow is only five feet beneath the surface of the water, and the remains are easily seen descending down, down, down into the dark, cold lake. The ship wreck hosted the first scuba divers on Lake Superior in the early 1950s. The Frigid Frogs were led by Jack, and their successors still haunt the wreck.

In the summer of 1987, Jack and I were on our habitual summer vacation aboard *Flying Dutchman*. We had been accompanied by friends in two other boats from our home port of the Sand Point Yacht Club in Duluth. After touring Silver Islet and the islands up to Rossport, we wound up at Isle Royale. We tied up on the north side of the Washington Harbor dock, seeking a bit of protection from a fresh southerly breeze. One by one, cruising sailboats from the Apostle Islands filled the south side and end of the big solid-timbered dock.

We had been trolling and were soon cooking our catch of milky trout and pink-fleshed salmon over hot coals on a grill ashore. As we passed the sailboaters on the dock, we greeted them; their words to us nasty stinkpotters were few and perfunctory. They visited cheerily back and forth from sailboat to sailboat, however, with beer cans and cocktail glasses in hand. For 25 years we had been sailboaters; we understood their selectiveness.

Jack and fellow cruiser Harvey Hengel both had a small pottery whistle in the shape of a loon, which reproduced the call of the loon, the distinctive bird of northern lakes. Jack proposed to go a ways up the shore, hide in the bushes, and answer the loon calls that Harvey would make from the dock. As soon as Jack was ensconced in the brush, 75 feet or so from the boats, Harvey strolled along the dock and informed the sailors lounging on their boats that he could call up loons. The partying boaters merely shrugged and continued with their libations. Harvey stood on the end of the dock and blew into his whistle, "Oooh Aaaah". . . Pause "Ooooh, Aaaah". . . and from the shore came an answering, "Ooooh, Aaaah!"

The sailors fairly leaped form their boats, congregating around Harvey, exclaiming, "He really can call the loons!" Impressed at last, since the loon is a shy and solitary bird by reputation.

The calls went back and forth for some time, then the skipper of the *Jolly Swagman*, an Australian by birth, declared scornfully, "He's got someone in the bushes with a whistle just like his, and he's no better at it than this guy is!"

With that the hidden loon came forth to everyone's great hilarity. Now powerboaters and sailboaters mixed freely, exchanging pieces of charcoal-broiled fish for

Australian beer, and had so much fun that the National Park Service ranger came down to the dock at 10:00 P.M. to tell us to be quiet so that the hikers in the Adirondack sheds on the hills surrounding the harbor could sleep!

Our favorite spots on Isle Royale are Chippewa Harbor on the southwest side and McCargoe's Cove on the northeast. Chippewa Harbor was a settlement of fishermen's families 90 years ago, but all trace of buildings has disappeared save for a tiny one-room schoolhouse. Wild and feral flowers mark the places where homes must have stood beside the pasture meadow. There is a long finger of deep water which punctures the island a good distance past the National Park Service dock. There is no dock there, but we've anchored at the end and have found it beautifully peaceful and well protected from wind of any direction. McCargoe's Cove, on the other hand, is the site of historic and prehistoric copper mines, and we always enjoy searching for them. Way down at the end of the inlet, it, too, is very protected from any kind of bad weather.

We knew Pete Edisen when he was still actively fishing near Tonkin Bay. Today his neat little house, fish-cleaning shack, and net-drying racks are a museum, part of the National Park Service project which has rebuilt a typical Isle Royale fishery. On one visit, when Pete was through cleaning his catch of the day, he went out onto the pebbly beach beside his dock to throw the fish guts to the seagulls. They came swooping down, fighting and screaming over the choicest tidbits, some landing on his head and shoulders, and a few settling there. Jack was amazed at this and asked Pete if the gulls ever left their ubiquitous waste products on him when they landed upon him. "Sure," was the good-natured answer, "If you're going to have friends, you have to let them do that to you once in a while." Jack has used this bit of wisdom many times since and has adopted it as his own philosophy of friendship.

Figure 38. Fish house on Wright Island today. (Jack Soetebier photograph.)

On our second visit to Isle Royale, in July, 1953, we landed at Ed Holte's dock on Wright Island on the south side of Isle Royale (Figure 38). We were trying to escape a sudden fog on the lake. Ed, who had been fishing all his life off Menagerie Reefs, as had his father before him, took Jack and our crew, two young boys, out to lift his nets the morning after we arrived. It was the highlight of the trip for them. His wife Ingeborg had been raised at Chippewa Harbor, where her father fished, and both she and Ed had many Isle Royale stories to tell. The Holte's invited us to their cabin, and Ingeborg played her small concertina (Figure 35); it made for a very festive evening for all of us. Ingeborg, who died in 1990, was a highly creative woman, painting driftwood during the long summer days while Ed was out fishing. She had amusing driftwood people and animals set up both in the cabin and outside among the flowers surrounding the house. A department store mannequin was seated in the corner of her front porch, keeping her company in this secluded spot. Ingeborg later became a well-known North Shore painter, and I am proud to say that we have her very first oil painting in our living room. Its subject is her summer home on Wright Island with the net-drying rack and the fog creeping in, exactly as it looked that July day we sneaked out of the fog to tie up beside it.

Chapter 9

Ontonagon

Ontonagon is situated on the fringe of the famous copper country of the Upper Peninsula of Michigan. Northeastward stretches the conglomerate rock of the Keweenaw Peninsula and points to the outflow of Lake Superior at Sault Ste. Marie. Westward lie the volcanic formations of the Geogebic iron-ore-rich ranges. But it is Ontonagon which named the notable copper boulder that resides in the Smithsonian Institution in Washington, D.C.

Millions of dollars worth of copper ore have been removed from the rocky finger of the Keweenaw, but the Ontonagon boulder was the largest piece of float copper known at the time it was removed from the banks of the Ontonagon River for public display (Figure 39). At the time of its voyage to the nation's capital in 1843, it officially weighed 3,700 pounds. It is believed to be an erratic, originating elsewhere and having been deposited by a glacier. It has been known for centuries. In 1766, Alexander Henry found the boulder in such a "pure and malleable state, that with an axe" he cut off

Figure 39. The Ontonagon Boulder on exhibit at the National Museum of Natural History, Washington, D.C. (National Museum of Natural History, Smithsonian Institution photograph 71–404.)

a portion weighing 100 pounds. Dr. Douglass Houghton, in 1840, secured a piece of the boulder weighing 25 pounds for study in his report on mineral resources of the new state of Michigan. Surely, over the years, the

Ojibway or their predecessors also had removed substantial amounts of the red metal from the boulder; it originally must have been far heavier than its weight as ultimately determined in Washington.

On our several trips by boat to the little harbor of Ontonagon, we had heard of the copper boulder, too. We wanted to see the spot where the boulder had once stood, so one hot summer day in 1963, Jack and I and Kurt, then 10 years old, made an expedition by small motor boat up the muddy Ontonagon River. Logs had been floated down the river for years to the paper mill on Lake Superior's shore at the town of Ontonagon. We found the going very tedious; we encountered many obstacles and had to detour many times around deadhead logs. Two or three times Jack had to replace the shear pins on our little outboard motor. After several hours of effort, we stopped on a mud flat to reassess our goal. Here, incidentally, we discovered bear tracks and a sedimentary rock with a beautifully preserved fossil—which I still have. We agreed to turn around, but not before Kurt, clad only in bathing trunks, had been enlarged to a size 12 by welt-sized mosquito bites.

Our small party was not the only one to have been defeated by the Ontonagon River. Lewis Cass, Michigan's Territorial Governor, led expeditions on Lake Superior in 1820 and 1826. The 1820 expedition had as one goal the locating and possible procurement of the already-famous copper boulder. Cass personally failed to reach the boulder because of the difficult journey up the river, but some members of his party did succeed. Others persevered. In 1831, Henry Rowe Schoolcraft, the ethnologist whose Ojibway tales inspired Longfellow's "Hiawatha", sent a contingent of his party to view the boulder. It took his group nine hours to reach the upstream location, a distance of 20 miles from the harbor to the site, and four hours to return. If only we had known this, we might never have set forth at all.

Chapter 10

Black River Harbor

We spent our 1972 vacation cruising aboard the *Hussar* with daughters Laura, Lynn, Gretchen, and Heidi as crew. Our son Kurt was off working that summer. We sailed Lake Superior for 10 days in the company of the Jack and Barbara Arnold family aboard their 32-foot fiberglass sloop *Waubojeeg*. We really enjoyed being together; not only did parents get along well, the Arnold children Jeffrey, Jenny and Jodi were the same ages as our girls and shared similar interests. Even our dog Cassidy chummed with their cock-a-poo.

We were returning along the south shore of Lake Superior. It was a beautiful summer's day—70 degrees, almost cloudless—a day such as we had dreamed of all winter long. If a flaw could have been attributed to that day, it would have been the wind; we couldn't seem to keep the sails full. The wind kept switching direction, all around the compass, and the crew, who would have loved to have lounged such a day away, had to keep adjusting sail trim and boat headings constantly.

Figure 40. Black River Harbor. (Jack Soetebier photograph.)

As we approached Black River Harbor, I suggested that we stop for a picnic (Figure 40). I wanted the Arnolds to see the lovely harbor spanned by a swinging bridge and its fascinating fossil and agate beach. We were anxious to be in the Apostle Islands by nightfall, but all agreed we could stop for an hour for lunch and sightsee as we picnicked. Before the hour was up, however, it began to sprinkle; our boats remained where we had tied them—at the gas dock on the western side of the harbor where the charter fishing fleet lines the side of the river along a sturdy boardwalk. The rain shower worsened and, with great thunder and lightning, soon became a downpour. The violent weather lasted all through the night. Records were broken. Eleven inches of water fell on the area in a 24-hour period.

Black River Harbor is surrounded by very high, steep-sloped hills covered with dense timber—in some places virgin pine forest. The Black River empties into it after cascading down a series of waterfalls between Bessemer and Lake Superior. By morning, a torrent of rushing water filled the harbor and churned on out into Superior at the conclusion of the Black River's precipitous 20 mile journey. The two Jacks decided that the river was flowing too swiftly for our boats to exit safely, so we waited for the current to subside somewhat before we departed. Several rock shelves lie along the river bank opposite the docks, and we were concerned about being driven into them once our boats were untethered. If we had known what was in store, we probably would have left at dawn, regardless of the velocity of the river current.

By 11:00 A.M., 50-foot trees, torn loose upstream during the night by the raging river, began arriving in the harbor. Some of these trees were coming perilously close to our sailboats at the dock. The skippers of the charter fishing boats began tying additional lines from their boats to the trees on the banks above the shore, and some of them even secured boat lines to the swinging bridge above their craft. Our skippers followed their example, took the extra precaution of running lines from the bows of our sailboats to anchors, which they implanted in the steep hillside beyond our dock.

Children and wives were ordered off our boats. We took sleeping bags, food, a portable radio, and a few items of clothing and went to the stone picnic shelter on the park grounds. We headquartered there for two days, sleeping on the picnic tables in the building at night, the children playing in the park all day.

We sat on the hill above the harbor watching the fascinating fury of nature. Giant timbers, thousands of branches—all came crashing, tumbling helter-skelter down the fast-flowing Black River. It seemed impossible that the fragile boats would be spared in this fury. In fact, one huge log did slam into the side of the fishing boat docked closest to the harbor mouth, punching a hole in it. The craft did not sink, although it shipped a goodly amount of water.

One of the fishermen took us in his car to see one of the waterfalls. The ground beside the falls actually trembled from the force of the water, and the trees tumbling over each other as they were carried furiously downward. The sound was deafening; we could not hear each other scream. The scene was awesome.

In one place, the torrents of rain had washed out the only road to the harbor, and a backhoe was soon engaged to repair the breach, from the town side. Since Jack Arnold had to be in Chicago the next day for an important meeting, my Jack called his mother and father, who lived 20 miles away, and they drove as far as possible down the Black River Harbor road. Jack Arnold was passed over the chasm in the road in the backhoe bucket and was then driven to the Ironwood airport.

That left 15-year-old Jeffrey Arnold as skipper of the good ship *Waubojeeg*. It was his responsibility to get her back to the dock at Bayfield with his mother and sisters as crew.

Late in the afternoon, Jack decided to try to get out of our prison, although the river was still flowing visibly fast. *Hussar's* crew cast off our many lines first; the boat shot out of the small entrance into Lake Superior; then Jack turned her and waited for *Waubojeeg*, communicating with Captain Jeff by radio. The crew let the lines go on *Waubojeeg*, and the young skipper headed his boat for the mouth of the river, neatly missing the two rock ledges to the east and handling the speed of the current superbly.

About a quarter of a mile out in the lake where the river current met the deep water, there was an accumulation of debris: trees, leaves, broken branches, all gathered where the river deposited it—a floating horizontal forest.

Jeffrey's initiation to manhood had taken five minutes. He surely had done a man's work that day.

Chapter 11

From the Head of the Lake to the Foot of It

In July, 1955, Jack and I headed for Isle Royale from Duluth aboard his father's boat *Viking*, beginning our two weeks vacation. We had departed after work, when it was already dark, and our boat had been struck by several pieces of the pulpwood which had escaped one of the mile-long log booms pulled across the lake in those days by tugboat. Jack decided to put in to Two Harbors for the night before we damaged our propellers or shafts and to begin our journey again in the morning when we would be able to see the debris.

Two Harbors in those days was primarily an iron-ore loading facility with several large ore docks and a cement breakwater. We tied up at the little dock used by the tugboats that serviced the ore boats in the harbor. In the morning we were given a tour of the tug on the other side of the dock from us, the *Edna G* (Figure 41). She is now retired and has been declared a National Historic Monument. She lies in her accustomed berth

Figure 41. The historic tug *Edna G* with taconite-ore-carrying rail cars atop loading dock at Two Harbors. (Jack Soetebier photograph.)

at the foot of the equally historic iron ore loading docks in Two Harbors. It was from these docks that the very first shipment of iron ore from Minnesota's famous Mesabi Range was shipped.

In the summer of 1988, we were invited to be guests of our friends Clint and Renee Ferner on the ship *Edwin H. Gott* (Figure 42). This 1,000-foot-long ore carrier, built in 1978, carries 61,000 long ton of taconite pellets, a kind of ore manufactured from lower grades of iron-bearing rock. She has bow thrusters, so she doesn't require tugboat assistance in docking or getting away from a dock, as ore boats did in 1955. It was the thrill of a lifetime for Jack and I to stand 60 feet up in the guest lounge, to watch this behemoth clear the breakwater at Two Harbors under her own slow, deliberate steam and head out

Figure 42. The 1,000-foot ore carrier *Edwin H. Gott*. (Thomas H. Mackay photograph.)

into the open lake. The feeling of a sailor is quite different walking the decks of a giant craft than it is clinging to the perpetually-heeled deck of a sailboat. So stable was the *Gott*, it was like walking on an island.

But the sunset off our stern horizon was no less beautiful when viewed from our small boats than from this great one. The grandeur of this largest of the Great Lakes is astounding, no matter what the condition of the water, or the viewer, for that matter.

Although, like the voyageurs, the Soetebiers need a week to travel from the head of the lake to the foot of it, the *Gott* needs only 24 hours. We, and the Frenchmen before us, put ashore each night in some congenial harbor to sleep—they beneath their overturned canoes, we upon our comfortable boat mattresses. The *Gott*, of course, moves continuously day and night at a steady

Figure 43. The *Edwin H. Gott* passing through Poe Lock, in the St. Mary's River, Michigan, with narrow two-and-one-half-foot clearance on either side. (Jack Soetebier photograph.)

15 miles per hour, thanks to her 19,500 horsepower diesel engines.

At Sault Ste. Marie, Jack and I held our breaths as the *Gott* slowly edged into the Poe locks at the foot of Superior, and indeed, the *Gott* just fit into the Poe with only 2.5 feet to spare on the sides (Figures 43-45). The

Figure 44. The deck of the *Edwin H. Gott*; people and shuffleboard court provide scale. (Jack Soetebier photograph.)

Figure 45. Full length of the deck of the *Edwin H. Gott*, looking toward bow. (Jack Soetebier photograph.)

new ore-carriers are built with the size of the locks in mind.

In 1853, the United States Congress donated 750,000 acres of public lands to a group of private financiers in exchange for the construction of a canal to by-pass the rapids of the St. Marys River at Sault St. Marie, enabling watercraft to move the 22-foot difference in height between Lake Superior and the river. Charles T. Harvey, the young superintendent of the project, is credited with building the Sault lock, a watery elevator through solid rock, within two years, and without the aid of modern machinery. The locks and gates he engineered were the largest in the country at the time. Harvey also chose the government lands to be exchanged for the financing of canal construction.

August Belmont was one of the investors who put up money for the lock in return for ownership of lands released by the United States government. That is how he came to own the land upon which the famous Calumet and Hecla copper mines developed. Born in Germany, Belmont was associated with the Rothschild banking house; he was married to the daughter of Commodore Nathaniel Perry. His estate "By the Sea" in Newport, Rhode Island, was built with money realized on the copper mines of the Upper Peninsula of Michigan. Although his estate no longer exists, his son's mansion, built in the style of a Louis XIII castle in 1894, can still be viewed in Newport, along with its gardens and artifacts from 28 countries. The size and opulence of the existing family estate in Newport gives an idea of the profits that were made on the copper originating in the Lake Superior area.

On the first day of the opening of the Sault lock in June 1855, the steamer Baltimore passed through it headed east with a cargo of copper (Figures 46 and 47). In the first year of the lock's operation 14,503 ton of freight passed through—3,196 ton of this total was cop-

Figure 46. The steamer *Cuyahoga* in the State Lock, Sault Ste. Marie, Michigan, in the 1860s. (Lake Superior Marine Museum photograph.)

Figure 47. Passing through the Poe Lock during the Trans-Superior Race in 1971. (Jack Soetebier photograph.)

per. While the government lands had been valued at $1.00 per acre, the actual costs of $999,800 for building the canal greatly exceeded that volume. However, by 1866 Calumet and Hecla and 33 other copper mines on the Keweenaw Peninsula were in production. Together they were producing 80 percent of the national output of the red metal. Meanwhile, by 1860, 114,400 ton of iron ore were being shipped annually through Sault Ste. Marie; the original canal was already becoming too small. By 1888, the Weitzel lock was added, and over the years, the MacArthur and the Poe locks accommodated the increased traffic. The Calumet and Hecla profited their investors greatly; as late as 1923, they paid a stock dividend of 700 percent.

The importance of the so-called Soo locks should not be underestimated. Although they were constructed with the knowledge of the copper in the area and the realization that ships capable of carrying heavy cargo would be needed to utilize that resource, their most important use came with the discovery of iron ore in Minnesota's Mesabi Range. By 1892, the first shipment of "red" gold left Two Harbors for smelting in Ohio. If iron ore had had to be shipped by rail, instead of going by water through the Soo locks, it might not have been economically feasible to develop the resource.

The rich ore of the open pit mines has been gone now for many years. But in the 1950s, taconite was developed. This is a kind of manufactured iron ore; low grade deposits of iron-bearing rock are crushed and mixed with other ingredients and formed into small pellets. Thousand-foot ore boats now carry taconite pellets to the ports of Gary, Indiana, and Conneaut, Ohio.

In 1959, the St. Lawrence Seaway—a system of locks and canals—was opened, joining the Great Lakes to the oceans of the world. This event brought good news and bad to Lake Superior. The good news was that ships from around the globe could reach the port of

Duluth/Superior with German Volkswagons and depart with Red River Valley wheat. The bad news was that the ocean-going salties brought the devastating sea lamprey and zebra mussels with them on their hulls or in ballast water. The lamprey reduced lake trout populations for many years before being brought under control. The zebra mussel's impact is still being discovered.

Today, although some general cargo passes through the Soo locks, taconite pellets and grain are the major products descending 22 feet on their way to the lower lakes, and 600 feet to the seas and the rest of the world.

Chapter 12

Rescue in the Susie Islands

On our way home from our summer vacation of 1987, Jack and I left the little harbor of Grand Portage aboard the *Flying Dutchman* and headed down the North Shore (Figure 48). Southwest winds had been building constantly as the morning wore on; about five miles out we weighed the risks and Jack turned the boat around. Bypassing the dock we had just left as too shallow for this particular wind and its accompanying waves, we headed for the Susie Islands (Figure 49). We knew a quiet cove, a little spot protected from winds from every direction except northeast, where we would have safe anchorage until the winds died down or changed direction.

As we slowed *Dutchman's* twin engines in order to throw out the anchor, we passed a small outboard boat pulled up on the rocks of one of the small islands in the archipelago. A young woman sitting near the boat waved to us as we motored by. After our boat had been securely tied down, Jack called out to her to ask if she needed help. No, she didn't. Her husband was on the

Figure 48. *Flying Dutchman*, our 38-foot steel Chris Craft Roamer, with East Duluth in background. (Jack Soetebier photograph.)

Figure 49. Across the Susie Islands. (Jack Soetebier photograph.)

island and would be back soon. Soon a man came out of the woods, the two of them got into the boat, and after a bit of tugging at the outboard motor, they headed out into the seas we had just fled. Within 15 minutes the outboard was back in the cove, and the couple putted it up to the *Dutchman*. There was about a foot of water in the bottom of their craft. The woman, beneath her freckles, and man, despite his swarthy complexion, were white as sheets used to be.

Jack tied a line from the small boat to *Dutchman's* stern cleat and invited the couple aboard. The young, adventurous couple, John and Sharon, were visiting from Atlanta, Georgia. When they heard that there was an historic copper mine on this particular island, they had rented the outboard from a marina on the mainland and set forth to explore it. They left the marina in the morning, while the winds were still light, and though they were amateur boaters, they had had no problems crossing to the islands. But as we could testify, the winds and waves had grown steadily all day, and now instead of gentle swells, seas of six and seven feet were crashing on the windward side rocks of the little island. The awed pair described how their little aluminum boat went straight up when it rounded the protective point of the island and met the full force of the open lake and the giant waves. When they turned around to return to our little cove, water had crashed into the boat. They had nothing with which to bail out water, not even a pop can! All they had been issued with the rented boat were two paddles, two life preservers, and one balky outboard motor.

"Well, just relax here with us," said Jack. "The wind usually diminishes around supper time. You'll be able to make it then." They took off their wet socks and shoes and we visited, with calming drinks in hand. Our galley had some chicken left, although we were nearing the end of our cruise and our rations, so I cooked a hot supper for us.

As the sun began to set, our new-found friends were anxious to leave, fearing that the marina would send a search party for them. Jack told them if it still looked bad out there on the exposed lake to return, we could easily put them up for the night. They got into their boat, started up the motor, again with much difficulty, and poked around the point of the island. But within minutes they were back. Jack radioed the marina that their customers were safe and would be spending the night aboard the *Flying Dutchman*. Then we made up the beds in the main salon and everyone tried to sleep. It was not easy to do; the wind was howling by now and the *Dutchman* was constantly moving. Jack had set both a bow and a stern anchor, since the holding ground in this cove was so rocky, and by midnight, *Dutchman* was riding them like a hobby horse, jerking and straining at first one anchor and then the other.

The wind had shifted to the only unprotected direction in this harbor—directly out of the northeast! Despite the fact that it was a heavily overcast night without a single star or moon to help light our exertions, Jack got up both anchors, started our engines, and slowly tried to motor out. It was hopeless, even with the boat's spotlight and John and I aiming flashlights at the shores; the night was simply too black to see where we were going. We narrowly missed the rock outcrop which guarded the point of the island. Jack decided that he knew where we had been, he couldn't see where he was going, so we headed back to original mooring place and threw out our big danforth.

Now riding on just a single hook, the *Dutchman* headed into the waves and rode them out for the remainder of the night. At first light, 4:30 or 5:00 A.M., we hauled up the anchor, cautiously rounded the rocky point, and headed the mile or so to Grand Portage—with the rented outboard trailing in some good-sized following seas. Without further mishap John and Sharon clambered into their little boat. We cast them off in the gray harbor, and Jack and I resumed our trip home.

John's parting words were "You saved our lives."

Jack said, "No, you could have stayed all night on the island until the waves died down."

"No," they both declared. "Not with the mosquitos . . . We would have made a run for it and probably capsized."

The Susie Islands weren't even on our itinerary that summer! Our new-found friends could say that day, as Charles Penny did after his 1840 circumnavigation of the lake, "Farewell, Lake Superior; we have shaken hands and parted in peace."

POSTSCRIPT

Superior Pursuit: Facts About the Greatest Great Lake[1]

by Howard Bell

Lake Superior has a calming fascination, whether you visit Minnesota's North Shore or live here year-round. From the sun shimmering calm of July to the gray crashing waves of November, the lake is a living presence that helps shape the climate, landscape, economy, and the quality of life along the shore. Here are a few facts about Lake Superior to help you appreciate the greatness of this inland sea.

Size

Lake Superior covers 31,280 square miles: the area covered by Massachusetts, Connecticut, Rhode Island, Vermont and New Hampshire combined. It's the greatest Great Lake, the largest lake in the world by surface area, and the second largest by volume. Mile-deep

Lake Baikal in Siberia contains the greatest volume of freshwater.

Drive the interstate between Chicago and Cleveland for a good idea of Lake Superior's length, 350 miles. Do the same between Duluth and Minneapolis for an appreciation of its width, 160 miles. If Lake Superior's shoreline was unraveled into a straight line highway, you could travel 1,826 miles from Duluth to Miami. It would take 2,531 ore ships placed end to end to form a line from Duluth to the eastern end of the lake at Sault Ste. Marie, Michigan.

Lake Superior is so big, it takes the sun 30 minutes to travel across the lake. As orange twilight fades to purple dusk at Sault Ste. Marie, the sun still casts long shadows in Duluth.

Lake Superior is also the deepest of the Great Lakes. Much of the shoreline drops off quickly and sharply to an average lake-wide depth of 489 feet. Along much of the North Shore, the lake depth drops to 700 feet within three miles of shore. The lake's deepest spot of 1,333 feet is forty miles off the Michigan shore near Munising. The world's tallest building, the Chicago Sears Tower, could fit in that hole, with only a few floors above water.

Creation

Lake Superior's creation is a two act drama: the first act volcanic, the second act glacial. The curtain opens 1.1 billion years ago, when the first sponges and other primitive forms of life were colonizing the planet.

Molten basalt erupted from a rift in the earth that extended near Thunder Bay, Ontario to Kansas. It's called the Mid-continent Rift, and like a wound that wouldn't heal, the rift bled lava for 100 million years until as much as a five mile thickness of lava accumulated. The movement of billions of tons of rock from underneath to on top of the earth's surface, caused the surface to gradually sink and form a broad shallow basin—the Superior Basin.

Had the Mid-continent Rift kept erupting, the North American continent would have split in two and Duluth today might be on an ocean instead of a lake. But the forces that fueled the rifting process mysteriously stopped, leaving behind the basalt covered North Shore we see today.

After the rifting stopped, the basin continued to sink. At the same time, the basin accumulated great depths of sand and mud eroded from nearby areas. But except for some river drainage, the Superior Basin remained dry and level until 1 million years ago, when a different kind of flow, glacial ice, began a series of advances that sculpted the basin to roughly its present shape.

By 11,500 years ago, the last glacial lobes receded northeastward and meltwater "ponded" to form Glacial Lake Duluth in what is now the western third of Lake Superior. Glacial Lake Duluth was 500 feet higher than the present lake. Today you can see remnants of beach, stream delta, and shore line cliff along Duluth's Skyline Drive, the "coast road" of Glacial Lake Duluth.

By 7,000 years ago, all the glacial ice had melted. Lake Duluth had become Lake Superior, filled to its present contours.

Water Budget

Just how much water is in Lake Superior? The lake contains three quadrillion gallons (3,000,000,000,000,000). That's ten percent of the world's fresh surface water—half of the water in the Great Lakes—enough water to flood Canada, the U.S., Mexico, and South America with one foot of water. A child born today would be 20 years old before the Mississippi River's flow into the Gulf of Mexico would equal the amount of water in Lake Superior.

Lake Superior's drainage basin is small for the size of the lake: 49,300 square miles compared to 1.2 million square miles for the Mississippi River. Each year, 2.5 feet of water falls directly on the lake as rain or snow. Two more feet enters the lake each year through streams or groundwater. The Nipigon River in Ontario and the St. Louis River at Duluth/Superior are the largest tributaries feeding the lake. Of the 4.5 feet of annual inflow, 1.6 feet evaporates each year and the rest feeds the lower Great Lakes through the St. Marys River. An annual average of 75,000 cubic feet of water per second flows out of Lake Superior into Lake Huron. That's about seven times the flow of the St. Louis River as it enters Lake Superior.

There has been much talk about diverting Great Lakes water to supply thirsty western states. But right now, water is actually being diverted into Lake Superior. Ontario's Okoki and Long Lac power generation diversions add a flow equivalent to the flow of the St. Louis River at its mouth.

Weather

Large bodies of water affect local weather, and with one-tenth of the world's fresh surface water, Lake Superior is no exception. The lake makes winters milder and summers cooler. The effect is strongest when the wind blows off the lake. The moderation is most pronounced along the hillsides that rise up out of the lake. It weakens "over the hill". In Duluth, gardens near the lake enjoy an average of 143 frost-free days, compared to 160 days in Minneapolis and 180 days in Chicago.

Gardens over the hill enjoy an average 123 frost-free days. But the warmer summer temperatures away from the lake allow more growth during the shorter growing season. Even over the hill, Duluth receives an average of only two days with temperatures in the nineties.

The lake effect delays spring and prolongs fall. Leafing and flowering can be slower along the hillside. And during May and June, when inland areas bask in spring sun, the lake shore may be shrouded in fog. Duluth gets an average of 50 days of heavy fog each year. The fog is caused when warm moist spring air flows out over the cool lake and condenses. The fog days have an appeal of their own, cloaking the shore in a chilly shroud with seagull cries, ship, and fog horns.

North Shore trees change color and lose their leaves a few days to a week later in the fall than the same species growing over the hill. North Shore falls are also known for their northeasters: gales of strong winds and driven rain caused by low pressure passing over Lake Superior. The majority of Lake Superior's 350 shipwrecks went down in fall gales.

The lake also moderates winter temperatures. Even over the hill temperatures rarely dip below minus 30 degrees F, whereas inland areas of Northern Minnesota can reach minus 45 degrees F. Lake effect snowfall is not as great as it is along windward Wisconsin and Michigan shores. In portions of Michigan's Upper Peninsula, 350 inches is common. Downtown Duluth gets an average of 55 inches. More snow, 75 inches, falls over the hill because more moisture condenses and falls when air rises to a higher elevation. The 800 foot difference in elevation means it may rain near the shore in early winter while it snows inland.

The winter of 1979 is the only period in recent memory that the lake's surface completely froze. The lake is iced from January through mid-April. Broken-up cake ice piles against windward shores often well into late April or May, when the temperature may be 70 degrees on shore.

Lake Superior does not have tides, but weather produces a tidal-like rise and fall called a seiche (saysh). Whereas gravitational pull of the sun and moon cause tides, persistent strong winds accompanying a high pressure system "pile-up" water against the lake's windward shore to begin a seiche. Like water in a pan that's been tipped then laid flat, the water rebounds to the opposite shore. The rise and fall sloshing of water continues after the weather conditions causing it have passed. Lake Superior seiches rarely affect the water level more than one foot.

Water Quality

Lake Superior is the cleanest, clearest, and coldest Great Lake. The average annual temperature is 40 degrees F; however, in summer, near shore surface temperatures reach 60 to 70 degrees F. Visibility of 50 to 75 feet is common. That's because Lake Superior has low concentrations of nutrients, suspended sediment, and organic material. The water is often cloudier at stream mouths, especially at the St. Louis River. After storms and on windy days, the water in the western tip of Lake Superior is often reddish-brown. The discoloration is not pollution. It's caused by natural erosion of the red clay shoreline in Wisconsin.

During the past fifteen years, improved treatment facilities have reduced municipal and industrial pollution in Lake Superior. Western Lake Superior used to contain asbestos fibers from taconite processing. The fibers have now been reduced by 90 to 95 percent. All North Shore community water supplies are free of the fibers.

Acid rain and snow does fall on Lake Superior but has not noticeably affected the lake. Nor do scientists consider it a serious problem for the near future.

Toxic pollution in Lake Superior is low compared to other Great Lakes, but toxics like PCBs, dieldrin, toxaphene, and DDT pose a threat because there is no practical way of getting rid of them, they remain in the lake sediments for a long time, and they can accumulate in the flesh of fish. Much of Lake Superior's toxic contamination comes from the atmosphere as dry fallout or in precipitation. Scientists believe some of the contaminants have been carried hundreds, even thousands of miles from their source.

Studies of lake trout in Western Lake Superior show decreases in DDT and PCBs. Dieldrin concentrations have always been low. Similarly, scientists over the past ten years have found less toxic material in Lake Superior herring gull eggs.

In 1983, Lake Superior lake trout were generally within the U.S. government safe eating limit for PCBs. Many lake trout in other Great Lakes exceed the limit.

Fish

Lake Superior's cold, clear water is poorly endowed with the nutrients necessary to support plant and animal life. Fewer nutrients and cold water means the lake supports a lower number of fish and fewer kinds of fish than other Great Lakes. Those fish also tend to grow slower. Some folks incorrectly believe that the more fish stocked in the lake, the more fish will be caught. But like all lakes, Superior contains enough food for only a limited number of fish.

What Lake Superior lacks in quantity, it makes up for in quality. Superior is the only Great Lake with an increasing population of naturally reproducing lake trout. Lake trout are an important sport and commercial fish which the parasitic sea lamprey virtually eliminated from the other Great Lakes. Unlike the other lakes, virtually all Superior fish are safe to eat according to federal guidelines.

Of the nine species of trout and salmon in Lake Superior, only two are native to the lake: lake trout and brook trout. Coho, chinook, pink and Atlantic salmon, brown and rainbow trout (steelhead), and a hybrid of brook trout and splake were either deliberately or accidentally introduced into the lake. Many of these fish do not reproduce well in the lake and must be stocked. Most experts agree that sportfishing is getting better on Lake Superior. Popular sportfishing techniques include shore casting for salmon and lake trout in spring and fall, and trolling the deeper water in summer.

The sea lamprey will always be a problem, but currently it is kept at a fraction of its peak mid-60s level of abundance. Lamprey are controlled by treating streams with a chemical called TFM that kills young lamprey.

There is some commercial fishing for lake herring, deep-water ciscoes, smelt, lake whitefish and lake trout in Lake Superior. In Minnesota, lake whitefish are only a minor part of the commercial harvest, and lake trout are taken in small numbers.

Economy

Lake Superior affects the North Shore economy as well as the climate. Shipping and water based recreation are major contributors to the regional economy.

Lake Superior is the headwater of the St. Lawrence Seaway, a transportation system that stretches from the Atlantic Ocean 2,343 miles, or a five day journey, across the continent to Duluth/Superior. In 1984, shipping activity contributed $233 million to the local economy.

Duluth/Superior is the largest U.S. port on the Great Lakes in terms of total tonnage handled and the largest inland seaport in the country. It is primarily a shipping port rather than a receiving port. Each year, over 2,000 international and domestic ships call on Duluth/Superior. Iron ore, grain, coal, and other bulk commodities are the primary cargos. During the shipping season from April 1 through late December, an average of 300 foreign vessels come to Duluth/Superior, primarily for grain bound for Europe, a fifteen day journey. Marble size pellets of iron ore called taconite comprise most of the tonnage shipped from Duluth/Superior. The taconite is bound for steel smelters along the lower Great Lakes, in such cities as Chicago, Cleveland, and Buffalo.

Lake Superior is the second largest freshwater resource in the world, but one of the least developed. Eighty-nine percent of the basin remains forested. It has only two metropolitan areas: Duluth/Superior and Thunder Bay, Ontario. About 558,000 people live within the U.S. part of the basin; 147,000 in Canada. The 206-mile North Shore from Duluth to the Canadian Border is home to about 105,000 people.

Minnesota's unspoiled shore is a big reason why tourism is a major part of the region's economy. In 1984, visitors to Duluth spent $63 million. Along the North Shore between Lester River (just beyond Duluth) and the Canadian border, tourists spent $24 million in 1981. That's 35 percent of total retail sales. Cook County, at the tip of Arrowhead, has the most tourist-dependent economy in Minnesota. Sightseeing, fishing, and pleasure boating are the primary reasons tourists visit the North Shore.

Lake Superior's crystal waters attract sailors, power boaters, and SCUBA divers. The Lake Superior boating season lasts six months, from May to October. The average sailboat in Lake Superior is 27 feet long; power boats average 22 feet. The open lake is usually too unpredictable for boats under 18 feet, although 14 to 16 foot boats are common in near-shore areas. In western Lake Superior between 1976 and 1984, the number of boats moored in western Lake Superior has increased 83 percent. In 1984, 1,356 boats were moored in seasonal slips along the North Shore. Pleasure, cruising, fishing, and family outings rank respectively as the primary reasons for boating in western Lake Superior.

Divers are attracted to the North Shore's craggy coasts, the final resting ground for five shipwrecks, all of which are near shore. Reefs festooned with lost fishing lures and interesting lava formations are other reasons to dive on the North Shore.

[1]Superior Advisory Note No. 19, July 1985 (Duluth: University of Minnesota Sea Grant Extension), 4 pp.

Bibliography

Barr, Elinor. 1988. Silver Islet: Striking it rich in Lake Superior. Toronto, Ontario: Natural Heritage/Natural History, Inc.

Bell, Howard. 1985. Superior pursuit: Facts about the greatest Great Lake. University of Minnesota Sea Grant Extension, Superior Advisory Notes No. 19.

Bogue, Margaret Beattie, and Virginia A. Palmer. 1979. Around the shores of Lake Superior: A guide to historic sites. Madison, Wisconsin: University of Wisconsin Sea Grant College Program.

Culme, John, and Nicholas Rayner. 1988. The jewels of the Duchess of Windsor. New York, NY: The Vendome Press, in association with Sotheby's.

Cyr, Donald L. 1978. Dragon treasures. Santa Barbara, California: Stonehenge Viewpoint.

Dewdney, Selwyn, and Kenneth E. Kidd. 1962. Indian rock paintings of the Great Lakes. Toronto, Ontario: University of Toronto Press, for the Quetico Foundation.

Fowle, Otto. 1925. Sault Ste. Marie and its great waterway. New York, New York: G. P. Putnam's Sons.

Griffin, James B. 1961. Lake Superior copper and the Indians: Miscellaneous Studies of Great Lakes Prehistory, Museum of Anthropology, University of Michigan, Anthropology Papers No. 17.

Holte, Ingeborg. 1984. Ingeborg's Isle Royale. Grand Marais, Minnesota: Women's Times Publishing.

Longstreth, T. Morris. 1924. The Lake Superior country. New York, New York: Century Company.

Marshall, James R. 1990. The sinking of the luxury yacht Gunilda. Lake Superior Magazine 12 (1:February-March): 48-55.

Nute, Grace Lee. 1944. Lake Superior. Indianapolis, Indiana: Bobbs-Merrill Company.

Penny, Charles W. 1970. North to Lake Superior. Marquette, Michigan: John M. Longyear Research Library.

Rapp, George, Jr. 1975. The archaeological field staff: The geologist. Journal of Field Archaeology 2: 229-237.

Rapp, George, Jr. 1979. Trace elements as a guide to the geographical source of tin ore: Smelting experiments. Pp. 59–63 in: A. Franklin, J. Olin and T. Wertime (eds.), The search for ancient tin. Smithsonian Institution.

Rapp, George, Jr., and John A. Gifford. 1982. Archaeological geology. American Scientist 70 (1:January-February):45–53.

Rapp, George, Jr., Eiler Henrickson, Michael Miller and Stanley Aschenbrenner. 1980. Trace-element fingerprinting as a guide to the geographic sources of native copper. Journal of Metals 32(1:January):35–45.

Stiff, John. 1973. Silver Islet: Cursed bonanza. Canadian Geographical Journal, 87(2: August):14–19.

Thurner, Arthur W. 1974. Calumet copper and people. Published by the author.

Tushingham, A. D. 1966. The Beardmore relics: Hoax or history? Toronto, Ontario: The Royal Ontario Museum. [Reprinted by Nipigon Historical Museum.]

Wolff, Julius R., Jr. The shipwrecks of Lake Superior. Duluth, Minnesota: Lake Superior Marine Museum Association, Inc., and Lake Superior Port Cities, Inc.